LIBRARY AND LEARNING RESOURCES CENTRE
Northern College, Barnsley. S75 3ET

i
p
c
mo

'A
of

de
by

Will the Leopard Change its Spots?

IOE Press

This book is dedicated with gratitude and affection to
Tony Edwards
my Commentator-in-Chief

Will the Leopard Change its Spots?

A new model of inspection for Ofsted

Frank Coffield

UCL Institute of Education Press

First published in 2017 by the UCL Institute of Education Press, University College London, 20 Bedford Way, London WC1H 0AL

www.ucl-ioe-press.com

British Library Cataloguing in Publication Data:
A catalogue record for this publication is available from the British Library

ISBNs
978-1-78277-213-2 (paperback)
978-1-78277-214-9 (PDF eBook)
978-1-78277-215-6 (ePub eBook)
978-1-78277-216-3 (Kindle eBook)

Typeset by Quadrant Infotech (India) Pvt Ltd
Printed by CPI Group (UK) Ltd, Croydon, CR0 4YY
Cover image THEPALMER/iStockphoto

Contents

List of tables

List of abbreviations

AfL	Assessment for Learning
AI	Appreciative Inquiry
ATL	Association of Teachers and Lecturers
CI	Chief Inspector
FE	Further Education
FEFC	Further Education Funding Council
HMI	Her Majesty's Inspectorate
JPD	Joint Practice Development
LA	Local Authority
LLE	Local Leader of Education
NCSL	National College for School Leadership
NLE	National Leader of Education
NLG	National Leader of Governance
NUT	National Union of Teachers
Ofsted	Office for Standards in Education
Ofstin	Office for Standards in Inspection
PL	Professional Learning
SEF	Self-evaluation form
TES	Times Educational Supplement
THE	Times Higher Education
TLA	Teaching, learning and assessment

Acknowledgements

Steven Pinker in *The Sense of Style* acknowledges the help and support of no fewer than 56 people. No wonder it is such a good book. I do not have so many people to thank, but I am indebted to what I call my 'community of discovery', my group of relatives, friends and fellow educators, who have drawn my attention to research, policies and arguments that were new to me, corrected my mistakes and pointed out omissions, weaknesses, excesses and inconsistencies. They have provided me with access to a relevant archive, encouraged me to reconsider certain judgements and to offer more convincing evidence for claims made. Above all, though, they have shown by their generosity with their time and ideas that we are part of something much bigger than any of us – we are part of the long revolution to create a more just, democratic and effective system of education in this country.

So my sincere thanks go out to: Emma, Tom and Charlotte Coffield, Dave Brockington, John Bynner, Jan Derrick, Tony Edwards, Michael Fielding, David Hargreaves, Bob and Sue Hyndland, John Lowe, Matthew O'Leary, Ro Pengelly, Joel Petrie, David Powell, Peter Tymms and Paul Wakeling.

There is one person, however, who has discussed every idea in this book with me and so saved me from making one *faux pas* after another and that is my wife, Mary, who has been my constant inspiration.

About the author

Frank Coffield retired in 2007 after 42 years in education, first as a teacher in a comprehensive and then in a boys' approved school in Scotland. He was also a lecturer in Education at Jordanhill College of Education in Glasgow and Keele University in Staffordshire, and Professor of Education at the Universities of Durham, Newcastle-upon-Tyne, and the Institute of Education, University of London. He was Director of the Economic and Social Research Council's Learning Society Programme from 1994 to 2000 and has written books on juvenile gangs in Glasgow, the so-called 'cycle of deprivation', drugs and young people, vandalism and graffiti, the impact of policy on the Learning and Skills sector, learning styles, and public-sector reform. Since his retirement he has written *Just Suppose Teaching and Learning Became the First Priority* (2008), *All You Ever Wanted to Know about Teaching and Learning but Were Too Cool to Ask* (2009), *Yes, But What Has Semmelweis Got To Do with My Professional Development as a Tutor?* (2010) and, with Bill Williamson, *From Exam Factories to Communities of Discovery: The democratic route* (2012). In 2014 he published *Beyond Bulimic Learning: Improving teaching in Further Education* (2014), with contributions from Cristina Costa, Walter Mueller, and John Webber. His most recent book, co-edited with Steve Higgins is John Dewey's *Democracy and Education: A British tribute*, published by IOE Press in 2016.

In 2016 Frank Coffield retired again from writing and speaking for three months and enjoyed it so much that he intends to retire every summer from now on. The views expressed in this book are those of the author and do not necessarily represent those of the University College Institute of Education, University of London, where Frank Coffield is an Emeritus Professor of Education. Stephen Leacock explained the meaning of the word 'emeritus' – 'from the Latin *e*, "out", and *meritus*, "so he ought to be"'.

Preface

Around 1783 Alexander von Humboldt, the 'first scientist to talk about harmful, human-induced climate change', was presented, while still a boy, to the Prussian king, Frederick the Great. He was asked 'if he planned to conquer the world like his namesake, Alexander the Great. Young Humboldt's answer was: "Yes, Sir, but with my head"' (Wulf, 2015: 5 and 14).

The parallel with Ofsted (the Office for Standards in Education, the Inspectorate) is worth drawing. For the first 25 years Ofsted sought to control the education system in England through power, fear and intimidation, just as Alexander the Great spread panic through Persia. But now, like Alexander von Humboldt, it has changed tack and wants to transform inspection by using its head, by using research like 'a plank in a shipwreck' (Wulf, 2015: 29).

This book seeks to encourage transformation by offering an alternative model of inspection – not a revision but a replacement of the current model. It starts with a clean sheet and a set of fundamental questions such as: does the present system of inspection do more harm than good? If so, what could we substitute it with? Why not an approach to inspection that draws on what we now know about how students, teachers, inspectors and whole systems learn best? How can we enhance the chances of a complete overhaul of how our schools and colleges are inspected?

This book necessarily criticizes the *status quo* but it is animated by a desire to replace it with a model of inspection that is more just, dignified and effective. The aim is to offer a first outline sketch of what an *alternative* model of inspection could look like, and I invite you, the reader, to help improve this first version by criticizing constructively what follows, so that together we could present Ofsted with a more formative approach to inspection, incorporating the most effective ideas, practices and policies, which already exist within the system. This first draft of a new model of inspection will also have to be tested independently of me and by a research outfit without connection to Ofsted, preferably in a small exploratory trial with a cluster of schools and colleges in two contrasting areas. To join the debate, to add your ideas and your dissatisfactions with mine, please email me at f.coffield@ucl.ac.uk

For those educators still subject to inspection, and even more for those students whose learning is, in my view, being adversely affected by the undesirable consequences of testing and inspection, we must build something better. This country post-Brexit will need an educational system that can rise to the enormous challenges it will face. Unintelligent accountability will damage our chances of creating such a system. Education is too important and too expensive to be evaluated by a model of inspection that is not fit for the future. If the new model encourages the emergence of a self-improving system, where, for example, inspectors set the ball rolling by exemplifying at all times the culture of learning that they seek to promote in others, then change – real change – will be in the air. Inspectors would once again become respected and trusted colleagues, acting as the cross-pollinators of challenging ideas and novel practices in a joint search with educators for improvement.

Executive summary

This book addresses three questions. Does Ofsted do more harm than good? Could we build a new model of inspection that draws on what we know about how students, educators, inspectors and whole systems learn best? What are the chances of reform?

After a brief history of Ofsted, which outlines its main policies and personalities, some myths perpetrated about and by Ofsted are dispelled. Chief of these is the guiding assumption that *the* most important factor in improving standards in education is leadership. Only problem – there is no hard evidence to back up this claim.

The research evidence is then examined to explore both the positive effects of inspection and its undesirable consequences. Three well-known and frequently cited articles from each side of the argument are studied in depth.

The benefits of inspection include: monitoring the quality of education nationally, regionally and institutionally; reporting on general themes such as the quality of maths teaching; setting and raising expectations; providing feedback and checking to see if it is acted on; involving parents, governors and the local community in the process; and challenging unquestioned assumptions, poor practices and incompetent teachers in the search for improvement.

Empirical studies have, however, concluded that the impact of inspection on student attainment is modest and indirect. Heavy criticism has been made of Ofsted's methodology, which has been shown to be invalid, unreliable and at times unjust. Among the unintended effects, educators are distracted from trying new curricula and teaching methods, towards meeting the ever-changing demands of Ofsted. Too many teachers have responded by 'gaming' the system, for example, by withdrawing weak students from exams. They feel under such pressure from Ofsted that they act in ways that they know are the antithesis of education by, for instance, putting the interests of their institution before those of their students. This cannot go on.

The descriptive studies of how educators have experienced inspection can be summed up in the phrase: inspection is felt as something done *to* them, not something done *with* them. What was introduced in 1992 as an additional level of change became in the wrong hands a hammer that has created a climate of fear. The most significant criticism of Ofsted, however, is that its methods do not reflect what we know about how learning best occurs or how change can be brought about in organizations and systems. For who is inspired to learn by being publicly humiliated? So the answer to the first question – does Ofsted do more harm than good? – is that the positive features of the present model need to be incorporated into a new approach that jettisons its damaging features.

The new model is underpinned by five principles that provide its moral purpose:

- Education is seen as inspiring the desire for continued, productive growth. Do our students leave school as lifelong learners?
- The fear that has been the predominant force for change is replaced by trust, which needs to be created, enhanced and regularly audited. How much trust do classroom teachers and managers have in Ofsted?
- Challenge matched by support. Inspectors must be free to question the school's view of itself, but unwelcome news is more likely to be acted on if it is accompanied by explicit offers of support.
- Dialogue is thought by senior managers to be the most useful aspect of inspection, but it must go beyond comfortable chats to allow for disagreement.
- Appreciative Inquiry rejects all deficit-based approaches and instead gives pride of place 'to everything that gives life to a system when it is most alive and at its exceptional best' (Cooperrider, 2012: 4). It builds on strengths, while seeking to minimize weaknesses.

The new model has nine components, each of which is accompanied by a bank of questions and which together make up a collaborative, formative and open-ended system:

- The number-one priority in education is teaching, learning and assessment that is not so much $T + L + A$ as $T \times L \times A$. Do students appreciate that assessment is one of their best hopes for intellectual growth? Do educators have an explicit theory of learning that they use to enhance their teaching?
- Professional learning is the main engine of improvement but some models are more effective than others. Do teachers learn new methods collaboratively with colleagues in school-based, peer-to-peer activities (such as Joint Practice Development) or are they still sharing, but not implementing, good practice?
- Democracy is *the* British value but our education institutions are run undemocratically. How would our FE colleges fare if judged against

Michael Fielding's (2016) six levels of deepening participation of students in their education? Or how would our schools cope if assessed against my six levels of participation by tutors? (Coffield, 2016).

- Does the present curriculum provide students with the knowledge and skills needed to tackle the main threats to our collective well-being such as climate change? It is Ofsted's duty to report on the state of education and yet it is silent on this central issue.

- Our schools have become exam factories and our FE colleges skills factories, but they need to become learning communities, where the creativity of every student and staff member is released, and where inspection covers all the rich activities schools offer and not just exam results.

- Inspection does not assess the resources available to the institution – a case of the elephant missing from the room. How does the college's resources compare locally, regionally, nationally?

- Context is not a backdrop but an active force that consists of the school's location, professional cultures, physical and material resources and external factors such as league tables and local labour markets. What is the unique combination of constraints and opportunities in this college?

- An overarching concern for improvement brings these components together with the objective of creating a mature self-improving school system. Does Ofsted have the expertise to monitor the building, maintenance (and occasional termination) of the partnerships that are evolving among schools?

The final chapter shows how these nine components could be operationalized in a way that would dispense with Ofsted's current four-point grading scale of 'outstanding' to 'inadequate'. A single adjective can never sum up all the complexities and diversity within a large FE college. A single global assessment is a statistical absurdity and the disappearance of spurious numbers would prevent the drawing up of league tables. The focus of inspection will also switch from a preoccupation with leadership to an equal focus on classroom teaching and management.

To deal with the accusation that inspectors arrive in schools to confirm their pre-judgements, access to data on exam results would be delayed until the new proformas on the nine components and a general commentary have been completed. A link inspector would be attached to the institution before, during and after inspection, and a college nominee would join the inspectors' meetings to prevent misinterpretations.

The inspectorate will need successful experience of teaching and managing in the toughest areas as well as the skills of interpreting statistics and research evidence, if they are to become specialists in evaluation. A democratic structure of national and local inspectors will be re-established. The multiple remits of Ofsted will have to be reduced and its independence guaranteed by making it a 'buffer' institution between government and the teaching profession. It will be given the statutory duty to explain publicly its response to honest feedback and to any fragmentation of the national system of education.

What are the chances of these reforms being enacted? They challenge Ofsted's culture and traditional patterns of working, and they have to be acceptable to senior civil servants and ministers. The proposals are, however, desirable, viable and achievable and likely to be widely supported by the teaching profession, despite being more exacting than the present system. They would reduce Ofsted's power but greatly increase its influence and effectiveness.

There are welcome signs within Ofsted of a willingness to listen and to learn from constructive criticism; some past misjudgements have already been reversed. The essential building blocks of a self-improving system are being put in place – hard-headed self-evaluation by schools and critical peer reviews – to which we need to add a reformed model of inspection. Such a model will enhance the learning capacity of the system, of Ofsted, of educators and, most importantly, of students. Britain – post-Brexit – will need nothing less.

Ofsted does not belong to the government, to the Department for Education or to the Inspectorate but to all of us. We have a right and a duty as citizens to review its performance and call for change. This is the essence of democracy – the freedom to think differently on behalf of others.

12 June 2017

Introduction

... it is tempting, if the only tool you have is a hammer, to treat everything as if it were a nail.

Maslow (1999)

The spark that rekindled my interest in inspection was an editorial in the *Guardian* of 2 December 2016 which claimed that Sir Michael Wilshaw, the outgoing (I almost said retiring) Chief Inspector, 'has ruffled a lot of the right feathers'. That rather favourable assessment prompted me to write a letter to the paper where I called upon Sir Michael to retract publicly his notorious claim: 'If anyone says to you that staff morale is at an all-time low, you know you are doing something right'. No retraction was forthcoming.

A few weeks later on 20 December 2016 an article in the *Guardian* by Laura McInerney discussed Sir Michael's 'mixed legacy' and quoted his wildly inaccurate remark, without evidence, that Further Education (FE) colleges were 'inadequate at best' (McInerney, 2016). I again wrote to the paper criticizing the excessive size and complexity of the current framework of inspection, which runs to 16 pages and needs explaining in a handbook of another 73 pages, making a total of 89. For a second time Sir Michael was invited to retract his remark about staff morale, quoted above. I am still waiting, but I am not holding my breath.

Other contributors to the letters page objected, for example, to Sir Michael 'arrogantly attributing the improved rating of primary schools to Ofsted's hard work [which] is simply insulting to teachers' (Evans, 2016). The occasional ill-judged remark by the Chief Inspector (CI) presents one level of difficulty, but Stephen Ball pointed out as far back as 1990 that the constant barrage of criticism directed at teachers amounts to nothing less than a 'discourse of derision' (Ball, 1990). What I find disturbing, however, about Sir Michael's comments about teachers during his five years as CI is their inconsistency. At one conference he would provoke and insult teachers, at the next he would lavish praise on them. As students of the practice of parenting know, one of the most ineffective ways of bringing up children is to swing from blame to praise so that they do not know what to expect and come to distrust the flattery as much as the recriminations. Within a short time children stop listening to their parents, and teachers reacted similarly to Sir Michael.

Ofsted needs a new start and, with the appointment in January 2017 of Amanda Spielman as CI, there is a possibility of real change. There is also an important distinction to be made between the behaviour of the CI (whoever that is) and that of the hundreds of sensitive and respectful inspectors, intent on doing a professional job, albeit within the internal hierarchy and strict parameters laid down by Ofsted. To encourage the process of change, I wrote an open letter to Amanda Spielman, published in the *Times Educational Supplement* (TES) on 20 January 2017 (Coffield, 2017), urging her to transform Ofsted from a feared incubus into a trusted catalyst of improvement. I briefly proposed an alternative approach based on seven topics and 71 attendant questions, the clear majority of which have never been asked by Ofsted. This book puts flesh on the bones of that short article.

Around the time the TES article appeared, I received an invitation to meet Sean Harford, the National Director at Ofsted. I went to the meeting with low expectations, but was pleasantly surprised at the number of controversial topics we agreed on. He was thoughtful, friendly and prepared to listen to serious criticisms of Ofsted. He detailed some of the changes he had already introduced, for example, reducing Ofsted's 400 pages of guidance to schools to 89 (still too high, I argued). He also attributed the need for such detailed advice to pressure from some headteachers who wanted to know exactly what Ofsted wanted from them. Yes, I countered, but was this not the predictable outcome of years of the 'high stakes' testing and inspection regime, which had reduced some teachers to serving up whatever they thought Ofsted wanted? We agreed that we were still some way from creating a self-improving system of schools and colleges. For instance, the teachers with whom I have discussed Ofsted's constantly changing demands tend to respond either with angry resentment at what they see as an attack on their professionalism, or with weary resignation at the extra work involved that distracts them from the learning needs of their students, or with an all-too-willing acceptance of the latest set of chains.

I left the meeting with the feeling that here was a senior figure within the Inspectorate who was prepared to discuss criticisms that cannot have been welcome, and perhaps those criticisms were couched, not in that English style of understatement, euphemism and circumlocution, but in a rather more blunt Scottish style of dealing directly with problems that, I would contend, provides more time for working out possible ways forward.[1] Sean Harford was also open to new ideas, which encouraged me to write

---

1   I leave others to defend the former approach; the latter sometimes treads on toes but it leaves no-one in any doubt about where the speaker stands.

this book in the hope of influencing minds and perhaps even practices within Ofsted.

At parting I offered to play the role of 'critical friend', with as much emphasis on the noun as the adjective, while being mindful of George Canning's stricture:

> But of all plagues, good Heav'n, thy wrath can send,
>
> Save, save, oh! save me, from the *Candid Friend*![2]

Inspection in England has become such a highly contentious issue that it may help if I explain my approach by answering Howard Becker's famous question: '*Whose side are we on?*' (Becker, 1967). I reject Becker's partisan approach and instead agree with Alvin Gouldner, who argued that researchers should not adopt the viewpoint of either the 'underdog' or the 'overdog'. It is not possible to do justice here to Gouldner's subtle argument, which supports a form of objectivity that 'consists in the capacity to know and to use … information inimical to our own desires and values', because of our concern for a larger public 'whose interests and needs transcend those of its component and contending factions' (Gouldner, 1968: 114 and 116).

To work within the moral framework provided by Gouldner means not siding with any of the main parties involved; not with the politicians, nor the inspectors, nor the Heads and Principals, nor the classroom teachers, nor the researchers, nor even the students. Rather, the aim is to fit the shifting perspectives of the leading players into one coherent and convincing story that does justice to all the main players, including the inspectors. No, especially the inspectors, as they are not allowed to answer criticisms publicly.

It means, for instance, challenging, when it is misapplied in education, the nostrum from business that 'the client or customer is king and is never wrong'. That mantra may work in the retail trade but it has no place in education, because students at times have to be told that they have misunderstood basic concepts in physics, biology or mathematics or that in the humanities they are still in thrall to naïve stereotypes.[3]

Similarly, students who announce that they are 'kinaesthetic learners' and who demand to be taught in a matching style, need to be informed that some teacher has badly misled them by getting them to complete a learning

---

2   Canning (1798). George Canning (1770–1827) was the Tory statesman, Foreign Secretary and briefly Prime Minister who fought a duel with Lord Castlereagh, a fellow member of the cabinet, and was wounded in the thigh. Modern politicians seem rather dull in comparison.

3   See Howard Gardner (1993) for more on this point.

style questionnaire that is neither reliable nor valid (Coffield *et al.*, 2004). As my old Professor of Education at Glasgow University, Stanley Nisbet, put it: the secret of assessment is to be able to criticize students' work fairly but firmly, and in such a supportive way that they accept that criticism, follow your advice and, as a result, your professional relationship with them is strengthened. This good advice to teachers applies equally to inspectors; it also applies to me for I hope to present Ofsted with constructive criticism in a way that encourages it to change.

The rest of this chapter will discuss the appropriate language for this task; the reasons for a new model of inspection based on educational principles; the intended publics for this book; the various rounds of critique and improvement which it has gone through; and finally, the tone to be adopted.

So far the main references have been to schools and my remarks are relevant, I hope, to primary schools and to all the rich variety of secondary schools, academies and 'free' schools in the modern educational landscape. I will also use examples from further and adult education, in order to pay appropriate attention to what has been aptly described as 'the neglected middle child' between schools and universities.

Up to this point the discussion has been about teachers, but I want to include in this discussion the huge variety of professionals who work in education and who are just as much affected by inspection.[4] To cover all those professionals working in the system the term 'educator' will be used from now on, to emphasize both the broad, liberating remit of education and the valuable, informal learning that takes place outside classrooms and workshops.[5]

The alternative model is also based explicitly on educational principles, where education is viewed as 'continued capacity for growth' (Dewey, 1916: 100) on the part of individuals, groups, systems and society. The model will reclaim not only the language of education and democracy but also the values and practices associated with them, which have been pushed aside by the invasion of the language, values and practices of business and management. One example: staff in FE colleges no longer talk of their Head of Department, but instead routinely refer to their 'line manager', a term borrowed from factory assembly lines. Why is this usage

---

4   I mean tutors, trainers, assessors, verifiers, support staff, mentors, managers, librarians, coaches, administrators, examiners, curriculum developers, governors, psychologists, outreach workers, youth workers, nurses and inspectors.
5   I will, however, from time to time refer to 'teachers' and 'tutors', and to 'schools' and 'colleges' for the sake of variety.

objectionable? First, it seeks to impose a hierarchy where before there were collegial relations between educators, at different levels but working, in the main, harmoniously together.[6] Second, it insinuates that the human interactions that are at the heart of education can be replaced with the mechanical relations between a line operator and the production of, say, Hotpoint dishwashers or Cadbury's Milk Tray. There is no equivalent of such a production line in education. George Orwell argued that the language we use can corrupt our thinking and our practice. Within the last 30 years the ways we think, talk and act as educators in England have changed and we have ended up in Jean Paul Sartre's phrase 'half victims, half accomplices' (Sartre, 1955: 189), because we have connived in those changes, partly by becoming fluent in, and unquestioning of, 'management speak'.[7]

---

6   I am not harking back to some imaginary golden age in education in the 1960s and 70s, but contending that relations between colleagues were more cordial then, because there was more time to discuss teaching, learning and assessment (TLA). Instead of the many centrifugal institutions we have now, where staff race for the exit to catch up with marking, lesson preparation and admin tasks at home, colleagues lingered in staffrooms to discuss how to get particular students to start studying. Of course there were arguments, colleagues who did not pull their weight and Heads of Department who were autocratic, but there was also a spirit of co-operation among teachers, which has become much diluted. David Hargreaves pointed out that a 'common weakness in poor departments can be the failure of the head of department to accept the responsibilities inherent in the role ... the appeal to collegiality is an excuse for abrogating responsibilities of a head of department'. Personal communication, March 2017.

7   The invasion of management-speak into education (for example 'the bottom line', 'key performance indicators', 'value for money', 'delivering excellence', 'consumers', 'products brought to market', 'inputs, throughputs and outputs', 'performance management', 'efficiency savings', 'branding', 'targets', 'quality control', 'high stakes testing', 'multiple funding streams' and 'learning outcomes'), has been so pervasive that it is now accepted parlance among educators, but the process has been relentless and seems impervious to criticism. We educators should resist by refusing to use any of these terms. Such a stance will cost nothing. I almost wrote 'cost neutral' which shows how successful this takeover by the language of business has been.

There is no suggestion here that educators have nothing to learn from the worlds of business and commerce. On the contrary, some of the central ideas that I have used in publications came from reading authors like Charles Handy, Peter Drucker, Robert Reich, Peter Senge, Piore and Sabel, Nonaka and Takeuchi. I learned from them, for instance, about the need to concentrate on the core business (in education, that is TLA); to release the creativity of all staff members, support staff every bit as much as teaching staff (how many technicians have been converted by University departments into lecturers?); and how to move from the tacit knowledge of individuals to new organizational knowledge (an ideal way of moulding the craft knowledge of classroom teachers into school policy). Practising teachers need to see for themselves the revolutionary changes taking place in industry so I used to take my higher degree students to view robotic technology at the Nissan factory near Sunderland. We then questioned whether *kaizen*, or continuous improvement, was an appropriate goal for education; for instance, are those colleges judged 'outstanding' by Ofsted expected to move on upwards to perfection? And then what? They could then spend their time, as Oscar Wilde's Mrs Cheveley advises, 'contemplating [their] perfections' (Wilde, 1966 edition: 213).

The main publics for this publication are clearly the Inspectorate, senior civil servants and politicians, as well as the teaching profession. The themes to be discussed, though, are of such general significance that they are relevant to parents, governors and all concerned citizens. I will at times, because the issues are so serious, introduce a lighter touch, as it helps to keep me sane.

Readers also need to know something about the processes this book has gone through. Once the first draft was completed it was sent for constructive criticism to my 'community of discovery'[8], a group of relatives, friends, former colleagues and professionals working at different levels within the system. Incorporated into my arguments are some of the ideas of teachers from all over the country who have taken the trouble to email me about being, as they termed it, 'Ofsted-ed'. Some of these exchanges have resulted in an extensive correspondence that has deepened my understanding. The aim is to produce neither a 'bottom-up' nor a 'top-down' model, but one that tries to see the system as a whole as it seeks to become self-improving. I also consulted the archive of Ofstin (the Office for Standards in Inspection), an independent group of academics, senior managers and classroom teachers, which was set up by Carol Fitz-Gibbon in the 1990s to reform Ofsted.

At my meeting with Sean Harford I offered to send him the penultimate version of this book to enable the Inspectorate to correct, without veto on the final text, any factual mistakes; to pinpoint what it would consider biases or misinterpretations; and to offer its verdict on my alternative model, its coherence, practicality and chances of being adopted. I duly sent the penultimate version to Sean Harford, who understandably did not accept that Ofsted's methods were either unreliable or damaging,

---

In sum, I am objecting to two unthinking assumptions: that business practices are everywhere and always superior to those developed within education; and that business has nothing to learn from education (the competition between schools for highly motivated students is now much keener than in many monopolistic industries). The wholescale penetration of business terms, practices and values in education has gone too far and needs to be reversed. As Stefan Collini argues, 'the fundamental model of the student as consumer is inimical to the purposes of education' (2017a: 107). Moreover, business in the main produces standardized, identical outputs by following simple rules and procedures, the very antithesis of the aim of education.

8   I prefer the inspirational term 'community of discovery' to the more usual, but rather prosaic, phrase 'community of practice': 'learners and educators must work together with democratic practices and values to discover new ways to address the main threats to our collective well-being' (Coffield and Williamson, 2012: 12). The word 'practice' also suggests repetition, whereas educators are about discovering new methods and ideas to improve students' learning.

but agreed that some aspects of my new model, especially the questions attached to each component, were worthy of further consideration.

One of my main concerns in writing this book is what tone to adopt. At one end of a continuum lie the dangers of bowing sycophantically to power – or of being naively accepting of the authorized version of events. At the other end, if the approach is too combative and oppositional, the powerful will dismiss the recommendations out of hand. There is, however, no comfort zone to be found between these two extreme positions. The offer of a viable alternative model will go some way to make amends for saying what government and Ofsted may not want to hear. What cannot be done is ignore evidence just because some in positions of power may find it discomfiting. Nor can the obvious, critical questions remain unasked, but such questions must be addressed to all sides in this debate.

The advice of Rosa Luxemburg will be followed: 'The most revolutionary thing one can do always is to proclaim loudly what is happening'.[9] I will try to be faithful to the spirit of that injunction by commenting without embellishment, without fear or favour, without bias shown to or against all the interested parties; and I did offer those most criticized – Ofsted – the right of reply, but not the last word. This is where constructive comments from my 'community of discovery' were helpful in pointing out excesses or blind spots of which I was not aware.

The rest of this book is organized as follows: Part 1 sets out the case for reform. One cannot call for a complete overhaul of a system without specifying in some detail why such a transformation is necessary. If you, the reader, are familiar with these criticisms, which have been made for years, then please proceed to Part 2, which will first list a number of general principles and then expound the nine themes that constitute the heart of my alternative system. Part 3 will operationalize the main components of the new model before discussing Ofsted's room for manoeuvre and a number of recommendations to turn my hopes into reality.

---

9   Quoted in Hind, 2008: 147. Rosa Luxemburg was a socialist of Polish-Jewish descent who co-founded with Karl Liebknecht the anti-war Spartacus League that organised an uprising in Berlin in 1919. They were both arrested and murdered while in police custody.

Part One

The case for reform

1

Chapter 1

A brief history of Ofsted: An optimistic tragedy in three acts

> *... the past is alive in the present. But the future is alive in the present too. The future is not some place we are going to, but an idea in our mind now. It is something we are creating, that in turn creates us.*
>
> Stephen Grosz (2013: 157)

There is no place in a short book such as this for even a brief history of English education since the 1980s.[1] On the other hand, accountability and Ofsted do not exist in a vacuum and are part of a particular historical concatenation of policies and personalities, the most significant of which need to be at least outlined if not discussed at length. I will necessarily have to be selective, with all the attendant dangers of bias in relation to inclusions and omissions, but this account was amended (by commentators before publication) when the amendment provided a fuller and fairer picture.

The relations over the last 30 years between the teaching profession and successive governments are presented as an optimistic tragedy in three acts, with the principal players each making a contribution to the downward spiral. I will be painting with a broad brush rather than giving chapter and verse for every twist in the plot. Act One of the tragedy opened with the Conservative government introducing, in response to what it alleged was a serious decline in educational standards, and to HMI surveys that exposed serious weaknesses in curriculum entitlement, the *Education Reform Act* of 1988. This fundamentally changed the power structure in education by limiting the functions of local education authorities and increasing centralization and the powers of the Secretary of State who took control over the national curriculum, backed by national assessment.[2] The first Act introduces the three levels of accountability: exam results and attainment levels for primary and secondary pupils were published; all schools were inspected regularly with the reports made publicly available; newspapers started printing league tables and those schools at the bottom were

---

1   Stephen Ball (2008) provides such a history from 1870 to 2008. Inspection in Scotland, Wales and Northern Ireland is a devolved responsibility and is there conducted very differently.

2   See Coffield and Edwards (1989) for a fuller account.

'named, shamed and blamed'. Inspecting every school proved to be a vast undertaking in a country with over 20,000 schools and in 2010–11 Ofsted carried out 24,559 inspections across its remit, which is much broader than just schools (Ofsted, 2012: 4). (See footnote 7, which lists the full remit.)

In Act Two some schools failed inspection, were re-inspected, and in the process began to haemorrhage morale, students and funding. Those considered incapable of improving were closed, senior managers and classroom teachers were dismissed and governing bodies were replaced. Fear replaced trust. A 'high-stakes' accountability and testing regime came to dominate, and the Inspectorate allowed itself to become the regime's drill sergeant; it 'put the stick about', as it enforced both the government-controlled curriculum and government-specified methods of teaching.[3] Distrust between government and teachers deepened even further when reports began to emerge of some teachers, so fearful of the career-ending consequences of failing an inspection, that they 'massaged' or falsified their students' test scores. Given the levels of apprehension and suspicion generated by school closures, such unprofessional cheating on the part of some teachers can be understood but not condoned.

The most engaging tragedies are those that interlace advances with setbacks. Some headteachers welcomed regular inspections because they strengthened their hand in pushing staff to change practices and focus more on learning than teaching, and they also exposed weak teaching and mediocre teachers. If the reports were favourable, staff morale was boosted and recruitment of staff and students picked up.

Her Majesty's Inspectors (HMI) provided such compelling evidence (DES, 1988) of the wide divergence across the country in the curricula that pupils were being offered that a national curriculum became necessary to ensure:

> the notion of entitlement to a high threshold of common knowledge, skills and understanding strong enough to provide powerful defences against those social and cultural pressures which exclude many pupils too early from vital areas of the curriculum.[4]

---

3   Gemma Moss records that 'Ofsted published 11 documents in 1997, 10 in 1998 and 326 by 2004' (2007a: 26); and that between 1996 and 2004 England's primary schools were inundated with 459 official texts on literacy alone, i.e. more than 57 a year and more than one a week. Hence the stories of special cupboards being built to store these documents, most of which were apparently not opened, never mind read (Moss, 2007b).

4   Tony Edwards (1989). The particular form that the National Curriculum finally took is a huge topic beyond the scope of this pamphlet; enough to say here that the case for a National Curriculum was convincingly made by HMI.

The greater focus that politicians and inspectors increasingly brought to bear on the work of teachers began a series of protracted controversies over teaching methods: for instance, what are the more effective ways of teaching reading? Examples of both good and bad practices began to be uncovered by the Inspectorate and by educational researchers. Guides have been published on *What Makes Great Teaching* (Coe *et al.*, 2014), some of the key ideas of which have been fed into the most recent Framework for Inspection but this approach has two serious weaknesses. The first is that effective teaching is defined as 'that which leads to improved student achievement' (Coe *et al.*, 2014: 2), which in practice boils down to better exam results. This is the central weakness of the school effectiveness movement in that education is reduced to what is most easily measured. Second, pedagogy is narrowly defined as 'the method and practice of teaching' (ibid.; 2014: 8). Compare that with Robin Alexander's definition, where pedagogy is 'the act of teaching together with the ideas, values and beliefs by which that act is informed, sustained and justified' (Alexander, 2008: 4). This extends the concept to cover what the culture values in teachers and national policy on their training and working conditions, as well as the complexities of the classroom.

What is still needed, however, is an equivalent guide to warn teachers off simple but spurious solutions to the complex problems of teaching, learning and assessment (TLA). I refer here to a growing list of fads that educators, under pressure to meet ever higher targets, have seized upon in the hope of quick and easy success – for instance, brain gym, fish oils, bottles of water, and using phonics to the exclusion of all other approaches to reading. It is not sufficient, apparently, to provide the evidence that learning styles are invalid, unreliable and have a negligible impact on practice (Coffield *et al.*, 2004). Such is their intuitive appeal that they continue to be used widely within education and medicine.[5] The more general point, however, is that there are in education bad practices that it is part of Ofsted's job to root out. Changing the ingrained practices of educators is an arduous task because teachers often employ strategies that are resistant to change.

In Act Two relations between educators and government hit rock bottom with ministers claiming (in my words) vindication for their actions,

---

5   A teacher approached me after a talk on learning styles instruments (Coffield, 2013). 'I accept your evidence that they're neither reliable nor valid, but I'm going to continue to use them.' FC 'Why's that?' 'Well, I've got about 500 copies up in my room so I don't want to waste so much paper.' I thought to say 'So you'd rather waste students' time by raising their expectations of being taught in the way they learn and then disappointing them', but – for once – I bit my tongue.

while at the same time generalizing from the behaviour of some misguided teachers to the whole profession: 'We told you so. Teachers cannot be trusted.' Further centralization and more rigorous accountability were the official response. The Office for Standards in Education (Ofsted) was set up in 1992 and the inspection of schools and colleges, organized on a three- to four-year cycle, was privatized to commercial firms who charged schools for inspection. The HMI, which had started as far back as 1839, did not disappear but their numbers and role were greatly curtailed.

The era of 'hyper-accountability', as Warwick Mansell called it (Mansell, 2007: 3), really took off, however, when the new Labour government began specifying in much greater detail how literacy and maths should be taught in primary schools. It also introduced the mantra of 'zero tolerance of failure', which played down the massive inequalities between inner-city schools and those in the shire counties.

Enter, stage left, 'deliverology', the strategy devised by Michael Barber who was appointed head of the Delivery Unit by the Prime Minister to 'drive up' standards. Was he successful? Barber and Mourshed claimed 'dramatic impact on student outcomes ... in just three years' (Barber and Mourshed, 2007: 27),[6] but Dylan Wiliam showed that, while test scores in literacy and maths improved modestly in the first year, before flatlining, test scores in science performed best of all without a national strategy telling teachers how to teach it (Wiliam, 2008). How come? Teachers had learned how to deal with the literacy and maths strategies and so became highly skilled at preparing their pupils to take tests, principally because the stakes had become so high. But what we really want to know is had their students' understanding of these subjects deepened? Peter Tymms carried out a detailed study into the official claim that standards had risen in English primary schools and concluded that changes to the curriculum and to the content of tests, together with teaching pupils to take tests and teaching to the test itself, vitiated attempts to monitor standards over time (Tymms, 2004).

Ofsted's remit was significantly enlarged in 2001 when *Children's Services and Skills* were added to its official title. The full list of the services it now inspects is daunting, with expertise required across the whole range from early years to education in prisons.[7] At the same time as its remit

---

6   Barber and Mourshed, 2007: 27. See Coffield, 2012b for a critique of the claims made by 'deliverology'.

7   The list is as follows: maintained schools and academies, some independent schools, early years and childcare, children's centres and homes, family centres, adoption and fostering services and agencies, Children and Family Court Advisory and Support Service,

was becoming wider and wider, the resources provided by government were being significantly reduced. Ofsted is being seriously over-stretched or is being set up for failure, or both.

I have yet to introduce the *dramatis personae* of this saga, which has been running almost as long as Agatha Christie's play *The Mousetrap*. Very different characters have played (with different emphases, style and success) the leading role of CI, including Mike Tomlinson, David Bell and Christine Gilbert. But the two who repeatedly hit the headlines were Chris Woodhead and Michael Wilshaw. The former will be remembered for his claim, extrapolated from inspection data, that there were 15,000 incompetent teachers in English schools. His period of office from 1994 to 2000 was marked by running battles with the teachers' unions over such general issues as progressive versus traditional teaching methods.

There were also public rows over particular cases such as his determination to overrule the unanimous judgement of his own senior inspectors by placing a school in special measures with all the damaging consequences of that decision for staff and pupils. His decision to countermand his own staff was revealed some years later by a request under the Freedom of Information Act (Smithers, 2005). The incoming New Labour government in 1997 could have dispensed with his services but he was confirmed in his post by the Prime Minister, Tony Blair.

Ofsted had only been in existence for a year before the first critical articles began to appear. Carol Fitz-Gibbon, for example, castigated Ofsted's methodology before a single inspection had been carried out and later in 1993 wrote 'with a concern bordering on anger' about the stress induced by Ofsted visits and the 'injustices being piled upon hard-working teachers' (Fitz-Gibbon, 1993a: 1 and 6). She found its methodology unreliable and invalid, she objected to the concept of a 'failing' school because of the considerable variability within a school or college, and she accurately predicted that a 'system which introduces fear … is a system which corrupts' and 'will lead to a distortion of data' (Fitz-Gibbon, 1993a: 3). She later set up Ofstin (The Office for Standards in Inspection), an independent group that organized conferences and published a series of academic reports and open letters to the press, calling for the reform of Ofsted, which was labelled a 'failing organisation' (Fitz-Gibbon, 1996: 21).

---

children's and school improvement services in local authorities, initial teacher training, FE colleges and 14–19 provision, work-based learning and skills training, adult and community learning, probation services and education and training in prisons and other secure establishments. It also assesses council children's services, and inspects services for children looked after, safe guarding and child protection (Ofsted, 2014: 6).

The relations between government and Ofsted on one side, and the teaching profession on the other, reached such a parlous state that, in my opinion, the word 'tragedy' should not be considered an exaggeration for effect; after all, the acrimony (of which more in the next chapter) was unnecessary and did nothing to improve students' learning. The tragedy has, however, recently taken an optimistic turn, which I shall explain shortly.

No quick overview of the work of Ofsted would be complete, however, without consulting the organization's literature, in order to find out what its leaders consider to be its main achievements. In 2013 a regional structure was introduced, placing eight regional directors 'closer to what is happening in their local areas' (Ofsted, 2014: 16). In his final speech as CI in December 2016, Sir Michael Wilshaw claimed that Ofsted 'has been one of the major drivers of improvement in education since its inception'. He then listed some of the significant improvements made by the system during his five-year tenure,[8] and I have made the following selection:

Primary school performance has improved dramatically, from 69% good or outstanding to 90% ...

Overall, the proportion of good and outstanding secondary schools has increased from 66% to 78% ...

This year alone we have identified more than 150 potentially illegal schools ...

We are not yet world class, but children and young people across the phases are getting a much better deal now than ever before ...

The only answer to feckless families is fiery leadership ... That's what I did at the schools I led and that's what truly great headteachers are doing now.

(Wilshaw, 2016, *passim*)

One puzzle that remains is why Ofsted's ratings improve year on year but the scores of English pupils in international tests such as the Programme

---

8   I have summarized the main points made by Sir Michael, but his speech contains lists of other significant improvements in, for example, early years providers and nurseries. Readers who want a fuller account should consult the speech (Wilshaw, 2016). FE Colleges, are, according to Sir Michael, still underperforming. For example, he mentions that in the year 2015–16, 12 were judged 'inadequate'. He comments: 'We can no longer afford to accept mediocrity on such a grand scale.' But 12 colleges out of a total of around 371 is 3.2 per cent. Seventy-one per cent of FE colleges were rated 'good' or 'outstanding' in the same year (Ofsted Annual Report, 2016). This is not sophisticated statistics; it is basic arithmetic.

for International Studies Assessment (PISA) decline.[9] An explanation could be that schools can improve the tests scores of their pupils and their position in the league tables without enhancing the quality of their pupils' understanding.

It is also difficult to disentangle in Sir Michael's speech what were the achievements of teachers and students, those of Ofsted, and those of Sir Michael himself. For a more nuanced account I turned to a speech by Sean Harford, Ofsted's National Director, in which he claimed that 'schools previously less than good are improving at a faster rate than ever before, partly as a result of strong collaboration between heads and HMI' (Harford, 2015: 2). What a pleasure to see those two words 'partly' and 'collaboration'.

Later in the same speech he expanded on this point:

> While Ofsted and the other levers of accountability have played an important part in raising standards, these achievements are down to the fact that we have the best generation of leaders working in our comprehensive schools, leading a very fine cohort of teachers.
>
> (Harford, 2015: 5)

He defended, however, Sir Michael's decision to remove the 'satisfactory' grade and replace it with 'requires improvement', because 'satisfactory' encouraged schools with favourable intakes to be complacent and rest on their laurels. This meant that, with a stroke of the pen, the meaning of 'satisfactory' was changed to 'unsatisfactory', and this new label was then attached to 28 per cent of schools which up until that point had thought they were good enough.

Another measure taken by Ofsted to improve quality and consistency in inspection was the purge in June 2015 of 1,200 Additional Inspectors employed by outside contractors (Vaughan, 2015). Reasons? According to Ofsted, some lacked the skill of writing reports, some were retiring, some did not possess the relevant qualifications or the experience of managing a school, while others still were not qualified teachers. But did these 1,200 do any damage to schools during the years they were inspecting? Was it really necessary for Sir Robin Bosher, Ofsted's director of quality and training, to try the patience of teachers by asserting that this severe cut in the number of inspectors did 'not equate to Ofsted being substandard up to this point'?

---

9   Other international tests – Progress in International Reading and Literacy Study (PIRLS) and Trends in International Mathematics and Science Study (TIMSS) – tell the same story.

(Vaughan, 2015). If they were not substandard, why were they sacked? Ofsted then moved quickly to 'bring the contracting of additional school and FE inspectors in-house', from September 2015, so that 'well over 70% of our … school inspectors will [in the future] be drawn from the ranks of current practitioners' (Harford, 2015: 3). Good; one large step in the right direction.

Ofsted also produces thematic reports on such general topics as the progress of able students from disadvantaged backgrounds and the deleterious impact on students' learning of low-level disruption. It also established a 'good' or 'best' practice database for teachers to consult, but this model of professional development has been seriously criticized (Hargreaves, 2012: 8–12; Coffield *et al.*, 2014, ch. 2). Short inspections were also introduced in 2015 to reduce the burden of inspection on 'good' schools and no doubt to save money. To my mind, however, the most significant advance is Ofsted's recently acquired but very welcome determination to play its part in the evolution 'towards a fully self-improving system' (Harford, 2015: 6).

The next task is to address the question: does inspection do more harm than good? Chapter 2 will start by dispelling some myths perpetrated about and by Ofsted, before discussing the positive and undesirable consequences of inspection. I shall attempt to do justice to both sides of the argument, by being equally critical of the claims made. One final reflection: a careful reading of the two speeches by Michael Wilshaw and Sean Harford reveals a decided difference in tone and content, with real, green shoots of hope for significant change by Ofsted in the latter's address. That is why this history has been called an optimistic tragedy.

Chapter 2

Does inspection do more harm than good?

> *... neither reform or change is in itself a guarantee of anything ... our concern is whether we can live with dignity in such a system, whether it serves people rather than people serving it.*
>
> Václav Havel, 1978: 18

2.1 Dispelling myths

Ofsted is used by some senior managers as the 'big bad wolf' to justify practices not required by the Inspectorate. In 2016 Ofsted published a list of such practices 'to dispel myths than can result in unnecessary workloads' (Ofsted, 2016a: 1). There is no requirement to:

- Provide individual lesson plans or self-evaluation in a specific format
- Use Ofsted's evaluation form to grade lessons or to undertake a specified amount of lesson observation
- Make available any 'specific frequency, type or volume of marking and feedback' (Ofsted, 2016a: 2)
- Offer evidence beyond that set out in the inspection handbook.

That final myth started alarm bells ringing in my head because, as pointed out in the Introduction, the handbook runs to 73 pages of detailed demands. This 'myth-busting' document ends by offering a glimpse of the iron fist in Ofsted's velvet glove by reminding educators that it still expects to see 'evidence on the monitoring of teaching and learning and its link to teachers' performance management and teachers' standards'.[1]

Matt O'Leary is concerned that, although Ofsted has indeed removed graded lesson observations from its inspection framework, senior managers are unlikely to change their mindset and working practices because they have become engrained. Instead O'Leary's edited collection of essays by practising teachers shows in rich detail how to 'reclaim observation as a

---

1   Ofsted, 2016a: 2. The standards 'define in 15 pages the minimum level of practice expected' of teachers and they deal with teaching (high expectations, good subject knowledge, ability to assess appropriately, etc) and personal and professional conduct (DfE, 2013). Should there not be an equivalent document on the minimum level of behaviour expected of inspectors?

medium on which to build sustainable, collaborative communities of teacher learning' (O'Leary, 2017: 6).

What is missing from the Ofsted document, however, are the myths that it would like you to believe about itself. First, Ofsted claims to report 'without fear or favour' (Ofsted, 2014: 4), but is it independent of government? This would be a rather tricky position to adopt when, for example, the focus of inspection changed one year from 'Equality, Diversity and Inclusion' to promoting 'British Values' the next. Who, may I ask, was responsible for that volte-face other than a government minister? This issue will be picked up again in the final chapter that will assess how much room for manoeuvre Ofsted has to reform itself.

A second myth which needs to be dispelled is Ofsted's claim that its methodology is reliable, valid and appropriate to the task. Sean Harford, for instance, argued that 'it is absolutely essential … that we apply the same principles and inspect by the same standards in every school in every part of the country' (Harford, 2015: 3). The evidence will be assessed later in this chapter, but for the moment consider the experience of a deputy head of a secondary school describing the training he received from Ofsted:

> In one observation of a lesson with fellow Ofsted trainees, a third of the room judged it as 'outstanding', a third judged the same lesson 'inadequate' and the remaining third did not know … By the end of the training, there were still jarring differences in trainees' judgements, yet the significant majority still passed the course.
>
> (Jones, 2017)

There is a third myth, which I wish to examine in depth because it is Ofsted's guiding assumption that has helped shape its notion of causality. It asserts without reference to evidence, that *the* most important factor in improving standards in education is leadership. Thousands of national and local leaders of education (NLEs and LLEs) and national leaders of governance (NLGs) have been appointed throughout England. In his first annual report as CI Michael Wilshaw devoted the first chapter to 'the importance of leadership at every level … When I look at any inspection report, my eyes are always drawn to comments on leadership because leaders are the key people … It is leadership that drives improvement' (Wilshaw, 2012: 9). No evidence is advanced for this proposition apart from his forceful conviction.

Which fairy sprinkled magic dust over heads and principals that turned them overnight into strategic leaders and chief executive officers? Would not a moment's reflection on the performance of educational leaders give pause for thought? Should the leadership qualities of Michael Gove, Nicky Morgan, Chris Woodhead or Michael Wilshaw be copied by heads and principals? Would it be a sign of successful teaching for an educator to boast: 'If anyone says to you that *student* morale is at an all-time low, you know you are doing something right'? The argument is not that leadership is often poor but that the expectation it will be transformational flies in the face of experience. In over 40 years in education, the leadership I encountered varied (with one exception) from uninspiring (competent at administration but hopeless with people) to authoritarian (often wrong but never in doubt) and success was achieved under all sorts of regime. So, an indiscriminate appeal to strong leadership as the most important single factor in success will not cut the mustard. What does research have to say?

Academic researchers offer a bewildering choice of leadership styles that range from transformational, to instructional, to integrated, to sustainable, to charismatic, to hybrid, to collaborative, to democratic, to systems, to ecosystems and distributed systems leadership. John MacBeath has even produced a taxonomy to separate out the six different forms of 'distributed leadership' in the field (MacBeath, 2009). So the first concern is that the concept is mired in conceptual confusion with each author supplying his or her own list of definitions, skills, characteristics, and implications for practice. As David Hartley has commented 'the concept of distributed leadership is – appropriately – all over the place' (Hartley, 2010a: 138). But worse is to follow.

Alma Harris, a leading exponent of research in this field, admitted in 2004:

> ... despite a wealth of school improvement literature advocating more collaborative and distributed forms of leadership, clear links with improved student outcomes have yet to be established.
>
> (Harris, 2004: 21)

There remains to this day no hard evidence of a direct causal relationship between any form of leadership and improved student attainment, although admittedly causal connections are notoriously difficult to establish in education. In 2006 the National College for School Leadership (NCSL) advanced *Seven strong claims about successful school leadership* (Leithwood et al., 2006) and by 2010 it was advancing no less than ten such claims (Day et al., 2010). The evidence produced, however, is far less compelling than these titles suggest, but they are widely quoted as if an incontrovertible fact had been established (see for example, Cheng Yong Tan, (Tan, 2016)). The second NCSL report admits that 'school leadership is second only to classroom teaching as an influence on pupil learning' (Day *et al.*, 2010: 3). But the reasonable inference that we should be investing more in classroom teachers is not drawn.

When the NCSL reports talk about improved pupil 'outcomes' they mean pupil motivation, attendance and behaviour. The direct link between leadership and improved attainment is the second weakest (out of 18 factors) in the quantitative analysis. It comes as no surprise that the organization whose *raison d'être* is to promote leadership in education published reports based on the accounts of heads about how successful their leadership was, but it has failed to produce hard evidence to support its case. Leadership remains one of a number of important factors implicated in educational success; it is not the magic potion that politicians and inspectors would have us believe.

One of the most extensive reports into the impact of headteachers on the performance and attitudes of pupils was conducted by Jeff Searle and Peter Tymms, who concluded: '... headteachers have little impact on the quality of learning and on the attitudes of pupils in their school, at least in the first five years of their appointment ... the most important thing in the school is the relationship between the teacher and the pupil' (Searle and Tymms, 2007: 41–2). Alison Wolf, reflecting on this research and on other studies in public sector management, delivered the following judgement:

> If we want to help schools with deprived student bodies probably the most important thing to provide is secure long-term additional funding rather than endless special initiatives, to help them to build up and keep teams of effective, experienced and well-paid teachers.
>
> (Wolf, 2007: 56)

Amen to that.

There are also some eloquent silences in this literature, which consist of the self-reported accounts of leaders claiming all sorts of positive effects, but there is virtually nothing that deals with the perspectives of their followers. The skills and roles of good followers are presumed to be so obvious as to not merit discussion: all they are required to do is follow. We simply do not know what it is like to be at the receiving end of 'distributed' or 'systems' leadership. Is it not possible that instead of the clear gains claimed by their leaders, followers see in distributed leadership either a highfalutin' term for the delegation of responsibilities, or the mere semblance of a devolution of power, or perhaps they have not noticed that leadership has been distributed?

Besides, who decides which powers are to be distributed and which are to be retained? How many guesses do you need? David Hartley is worth quoting again, about the rhetoric on leadership running ahead of the evidence: 'The asymmetries of power which suffuse the practice of distributed leadership remain hidden and unexplained ... who distributes what, to whom, for how long, and to what end are all political, moral and ethical questions' (Hartley, 2010b: 279) that tend not to be addressed.

One final difficulty. For decades ministers from the main political parties have governed via command and control, yet at the same time they have preached the virtues of distributed leadership to the public services. What are the chances of us creating a mature, self-improving education system when ministers and senior civil servants hoard power (for example, in the formation and evaluation of policy) while insisting that those in the middle tiers of management distribute it? Leadership should not be accorded the status of a 'magic silver bullet from a silver gun', because it may be firing blanks for all we know. Or more likely, the bullet fails to strike its target directly, ricochets off anything in its way and its impact peters out.

Cheng Yong Tan has examined two types of mediating influences. First, the external challenges presented by, say, the abilities and prior attainment of students. Second, the internal constraints of, say, low teacher morale. He concluded that 'the cross-sectional nature of [such] data ... precludes any definitive claims of causation between principal leadership and student achievement'. He even found 'a negative relationship between distributed leadership and student achievement (albeit for *Disadvantaged* students only)' (Tan, 2016: 17. Original emphasis). Time to move on.

2.2 The positive effects of inspection

Ofsted seeks to provide fair, impartial, authoritative and comparable judgements about the quality of 'providers, local areas and national standards to help inform' (Ofsted, 2014: 6) the choices made by parents, students and employers. It highlights areas of strength and weakness and has revealed underperformance in some regions and in children from disadvantaged backgrounds, including able children from such backgrounds. There is also a need for 'an independent and watchful eye' that will 'monitor, challenge and support providers that are not yet good to ensure that they are improving' (Ofsted, 2014: 4 and 11).

Other possible benefits of inspection include: creating a greater sense of *esprit de corps* among educators (and binding new teachers into the team) when faced with external evaluation; acting as a stimulus to update policies; checking on the adequacy of provision, say, for students with special educational needs; making necessary changes that have been constantly postponed; and pulling managers together behind the plan to address the weaknesses identified by inspectors.

For Sean Harford, the primary purpose of inspection 'will always be to champion the right of every child to a decent education' (Harford, 2015: 6). The job of an inspector is 'to make unpopular decisions, challenge the status quo and tackle vested interests in the relentless pursuit of higher standards' (Harford, 2015: 2). Ofsted has also forced some schools and colleges to face up to difficult issues such as bullying, inadequate teaching or poor transition arrangements that demotivate primary pupils when they move to secondary schools. Uncomfortable messages have also been passed to some faith schools – Christian, Jewish and Muslim – to ensure that all schools promote diversity, tolerance and respect for others. Ofsted's willingness to act without fear or favour was demonstrated by putting some so-called 'free' schools into special measures and some were closed down.

Ofsted has also helped to eliminate bad practices and poor teaching; it has raised expectations of what students can achieve and given heads and principals skills, knowledge and insights into their institutions. Dialogue between inspectors and classroom teachers can also render teaching explicit and so open to discussion and improvement. Janet Ouston and Jacqueline Davies showed that constructive discussions tended to take place in what they called 'reflective' schools, where staff already understood their strengths and weaknesses, were professionally confident and 'did not allow the inspection to intimidate them' (Ouston and Davies, 1998: 24).

Having immersed myself in the literature on the beneficial and the undesirable effects of inspection, I noticed that commentators on both sides of the argument tended to exhibit, not an obvious, but a subtle bias in favour of the position they supported. So, for example, the limitations of their research would be mentioned but played down, while its strengths were unduly emphasized; and inconvenient data would be filtered out. The impression created was of authors so committed to their cause that research became the hunt for evidence to support the prejudices they had started with.

Have we blundered with Alice into Wonderland where sentence comes before verdict? No, something more prosaic and commonplace is at play here. The inability to spot bias in one's own work seems pretty universal. Rather than viewing unintentional bias as a deliberate attempt to deceive, it is better seen as part of the struggle in which we are all involved, to be objective, 'a struggle with demands more than the mere application of technical standards alone ... something more than a belief in reliability or validity' (Gouldner, 1968: 116).

Articles written by Ofsted or by ex-inspectors, for instance, conclude that inspection improves the quality of education despite the manifest (and admitted) weaknesses in their methodology. Similarly, some critics of Ofsted reveal their lack of objectivity by using such terms as 'the poison in the system' (Fitz-Gibbon and Stephenson, 1996: 16) or by claiming that Ofsted 'assumes the school workforce is inherently lazy and is only motivated by fear of reprisal' (Brookes, 2008: 93). I have interrogated the evidence on both sides of the divide and selected reports that appeared even-handed, which acknowledged alternative interpretations and which showed awareness of possible biases. It usually takes, however, a political opponent to spot the beam in one's own eye.

2.2.1 Survival of the weakest

This book does not claim to present a comprehensive study of the vast literature on inspection. Instead, I have chosen, for reasons of space, three well-known and frequently cited articles from each side of the controversy that will bring into the open most of the complexities involved.

The first article that supports improvement concluded that those schools identified as 'least effective' sustained improvement more than those categorized as 'more effective but with serious weaknesses'. The first author, Peter Matthews, is a former HMI and the second, Pam Sammons, worked as a consultant for Ofsted. Together they wrote what they described as 'the major evaluation of the impact of Ofsted' which found that:

> inspection has played an important role as a catalyst for change and improvement during the 10-year period 1993–2003, particularly for weaker schools. Over one million students were estimated to have benefited from improvements in the quality of education provided by schools which moved out of special measures and substantially larger numbers from improvements in schools with serious weaknesses during this period.
>
> (Matthews and Sammons, 2005: 162)

These are substantial achievements that should be widely acknowledged, and the finding about the differential effectiveness of inspection, with the least effective schools making greater progress than those judged to be more effective, is intriguing.

When the authors turn to explaining this finding, however, they fail to discuss any alternative interpretations, despite providing the necessary data.

The differential improvement is accounted for by 'core leadership', which they point out HMI identified as far back as 1977 as 'the most important single factor associated with the success of "good schools"' (Matthews and Sammons, 2005: 168). For 50 years this judgement has dominated the culture of the Inspectorate, but the only evidence advanced, apart from the testimony of inspectors, is a small number of case studies where headteachers convinced researchers that their leadership was the vital ingredient in their success. But what we need to know is: can an 'outstanding leader' of a school in a leafy suburb transform a 'failing school' with a very different intake, social context and set of teachers?

Matthews and Sammons also reported that the least effective schools had shown marked improvement in national tests and in the quality of teaching; achievements surely of classroom teachers and students, neither of whom merit a mention. These schools had also received greater resources and extra support, which help to explain their superior level of improvement. The authors commented further on the close relationship between the quality of leadership and the quality of self-evaluation; but is that not exactly what one would expect, given that the latter is written by the former? My argument remains that leadership is a necessary but not a sufficient cause of improvement.

There is, moreover, no criticism made in their article of the literature on leadership or of the succession of inspection frameworks; no questioning of the concept of a 'failing' secondary school, although research has revealed considerable variability within schools, from department to department; and the high percentages of pupils on free school meals in secondary schools in special measures[2] are presented without reflecting that Ofsted may be failing to make allowances for the difficulties of teaching in such schools. The fact that 1,451 (primary, secondary and special) schools were placed in special measures over the period 1993–2004, 220 of which were later closed, is recorded without comment. Those at the sharp end of these decisions will be quoted shortly, but is it not incumbent on commentators to acknowledge human suffering, especially if your organization made the decision to close?

2.2.2 Ofsted's reliability
The second article is a contribution from Ofsted on the reliability of its new short inspections of 'good' schools, carried out by one or two inspectors, lasting one day, every three years. It is encouraging to see Ofsted studying the reliability of its own procedures by investigating how often two inspectors

---

2   Twenty-one per cent with more than 20 per cent and a further 18 per cent with more than 35 per cent.

conducting an inspection of the same school on the same day come to the same conclusions. The key finding was that 'the inter-observer agreement between the independent inspectors was relatively strong. In 22 of the 24 completed inspections, inspectors agreed on their final decisions' (Ofsted, 2017: 6). This suggests a high degree of reliability.

The limitations of this small-scale, exploratory study are spelled out:

> only good primary schools [of between 250–500 pupils] involving HMI ... were considered. Alongside the small number of inspections that were eventually carried out [24 out of 24,000 schools or 0.1%], this means that the results of the study should not be generalized more broadly, particularly to reflect the reliability of all types of Ofsted school inspection.
>
> (Ofsted, 2017: 24)

The new CI, Amanda Spielman, announced these findings thus:

> The study provides a welcome positive view of inspector consistency ... These findings should provide some re-assurance that the purpose of the short-inspection model is being met, and that inspectors made consistent judgements.
>
> (*Times Education Supplement*, 7 March 2017)

Is this not exactly the kind of generalization that the report warned against?

Questions also need to be asked about the 'independence' of these inspections. Two of the four 'independent' observers, whose job it was to check that the two inspectors worked independently of each other, were former HMI. Besides, the inspectors received the same pre-inspection data about the schools and are likely to have formed a view. Both inspectors also attended at the start of the day the same meeting with the senior managers of the school. In one case, however, 'both inspectors were in the same room and listened to the same evidence from the school's leader and each formed different perceptions of the quality of school leadership' (Ofsted, 2017: 32). Inspection is based on subjective judgements that are then turned into seemingly objective data.

Even if the inspectors had achieved 100 per cent reliability, their agreement would only have established consistency, not validity which is the more important concept. The two inspectors could have been operating like two archers, both of whom were consistently firing arrow after arrow, metres to the right of the target. The report claimed strong agreement between the pairs of inspector, but it is silent on the identification of effective teaching. As the report itself acknowledges, we still do not know: would the same effects be found with Ofsted inspectors rather than HMI? Or with large, complex FE colleges rather than more homogeneous primary schools with fewer specializations? The report did, however, prompt this question: are the processes that are inspected those that lead to the most improvement?

2.2.3 The impact of inspection

Ofsted argues that it 'gets it right most of the time' (Harford, 2015: 3) and points to the evidence provided by a survey – the third study to be evaluated – it conducted into the views of school leaders on the impact of inspection. It found that 82 per cent agreed that 'the benefits of inspection outweigh the pressures' and that 'the demands of being inspected were reasonable and that the judgements were fair and accurate' (Ofsted, 2014: 1). The school leaders also reported that the most helpful aspect of inspection was professional dialogue with the inspectors, more helpful than feedback or recommendations for improvement. Written comments from the leaders also mentioned other benefits, with one newly appointed head reporting that inspection gave him a mandate for change and another that it gave the senior management team confidence in their judgements and improvement plans.

The survey also found that schools judged 'outstanding' found their inspection report helpful, while those judged 'inadequate' were more negative, with 41 per cent of the latter recording that the pressures outweighed the benefits. Who knew? This online survey presented the views of school leaders who were feeding back their reactions to the same organization which will return to inspect them in the future, so the unequal distribution of power may help to explain the high levels of satisfaction. That opinion is supported by Mick Brookes, formerly General Secretary of the National Association of Head Teachers, who wrote of colleagues 'so traumatized by the experience [of inspection] that they simply want to forget it, and hence don't complain to Ofsted – only to us'. (Brookes, 2008: 87). So the question remains: would independent researchers obtain the same results? That replication study needs to be done.

Desirable outcomes of inspection appear to be: society benefits from nationwide evidence on the quality of education and from educational institutions being held to account for the vast sums of taxpayers' money spent on them. The budget in March 2017 allocated £402 billion to education for 2017–18. The feedback that Ofsted provides each institution, on its strengths and weaknesses, is designed to encourage improvement, but for this mechanism to be effective those inspected have to agree that the feedback is accurate, and they have to act on it. By publishing its reports Ofsted also increases the pressure on educators to improve, as students, parents, governors, local politicians and the media begin to clamour for change. By issuing a detailed handbook of inspection, Ofsted makes explicit its expectations and the minimal thresholds of acceptability.

To these multiple tasks Herbert Altrichter and David Kemethofer have added another, namely that new inspection systems are developing an 'independent expert role' (Altrichter and Kemethofer, 2015: 33), where inspectors seek to become the professional specialists in evaluation through their up-to-date knowledge of educational research. When Ofsted started work, commentators questioned whether it could sensibly combine the twin purposes of accountability and improvement. What are its chances of fulfilling all the above roles, given that it has also undergone a major extension of its remit as well as a serious reduction in its funding? A further problem is that the more pressure Ofsted applies, the more unintended (but highly predictable) consequences appear. To these I now turn.

2.3 The undesirable consequences of inspection
2.3.1 A case study
In 2014 I received from a team leader in Maths at a comprehensive school a 21-page missive that analysed her experience of inspection. Her department and school were awarded the second lowest category, 'requires improvement'. She made many serious criticisms of Ofsted's methods, only one of which I have space to expound here. It detailed the evidence base for that poor assessment: eight lessons were graded by the same inspector (some observed for 20 minutes, the rest for one hour and five minutes). That amounted to 0.1 per cent of the total number of lessons taught by 20+ teachers in her department in the academic year in question. When the five lessons that were briefly observed but not graded were added, the percentage of lessons observed rose to 0.16. Her report concluded:

> The evidence collected was neither sufficient in quantity nor sufficiently representative to enable a secure assessment of the quality of teaching and learning ... teachers will increasingly move from a position of healthy scepticism to an attitude of cynicism [and] will increasingly work according to what they perceive to be their own narrow self-interest (including the boosting of exam results by hook or by crook) rather than a genuine interest in the education of the students they teach.[3]

---

3   Personal communication from the head of the maths department, 2014.

What gives her report such force is the pervasive sense of injustice, which was not directed at the inspector in question who was described as 'professional, efficient and competent', but at Ofsted's unreliable and invalid methodology. The sample was too small, unrepresentative, and observed by only one inspector to bear the weight of the conclusions drawn. Placing such trust in the judgement of one inspector could be described as Ofsted's doctrine of the immaculate perception.

The outcome for the school, according to the headteacher, was 'incredibly demotivating to staff and may put off students coming here',[4] even though its pass rate was well above the national average and much higher than any other regional or local school. How then to explain the poor grade? The overall exam results were lower than in the previous year, mainly because the school takes its mission of inclusion seriously and enrols students who do not have English as a first language, or who have serious personal, educational and social problems, or who are working part-time more than 15 hours per week to help support their family. The headteacher also mentioned the huge pressures placed on senior managers, who have to lift their colleagues after an inspection they regard as punitive rather than constructive.

Is this case atypical? Anything but. Anastasia de Waal edited a collection of nine essays on the impact of inspection and concluded that '... the quality of the school, as it is gauged by Ofsted, hangs largely on how the school is performing in national examinations' (de Waal, 2008). One of her contributors, Warwick Mansell, went further by arguing that inspection grades hinge on test and exam results to the virtual exclusion of qualitative evidence about, say, the breadth of the curriculum on offer or extra-curricular activities. Here is his summation:

> Ofsted visited 6,331 primaries in 2006–07 ... of these, 98 per cent had the same inspection verdict overall as they had for 'achievement and standards' ... Among secondary schools, the apparent link between exam results and the overall verdict was almost as strong, with 96 per cent gaining the same summing-up judgement as they were awarded on 'achievement and standards'.... In not one school of the 7,612 visited that year did the overall judgement differ by more than a single grade from that given to a school on the basis of its results.
>
> (Mansell, 2008: 57–8)

---

4   Personal communication from the Headteacher of the school, 2016.

The charge levelled at Ofsted's methods is a serious one: namely, that reading a school's previous inspection report and familiarizing themselves with its exam results leads inspectors to prejudge the school so that they select the evidence needed to support that prejudice. What is there to prevent an inspector from so acting? Exam results are used as a poor proxy for the quality of TLA, as if there were a direct causal connection between the latter and the former. But there are numerous other factors that need to be taken into account, for example, the abilities and prior achievements of the intake of students; the high mobility of students moving from school to school[5]; students who are determined to do well despite what they consider to be substandard teaching; private tuition that some families can afford; and the test results themselves are unreliable and vulnerable to being manipulated by teaching to the test and concentrating on the skills of passing exams.

Why have test and exam results become the main criterion for judging quality? Partly because exam data looks more objective than subjective observations, although Ofsted inspectors have been consistently criticized for presenting even their subjective impressions as if they were objective information. In the modern world data drives everything and the regime of numbers has extended the reach and significance of surveillance. This fixation with data suffers from two serious flaws. First, much of the data on which so much rests is unreliable and invalid. Trends in progress can no longer be established because of changes to the curriculum, to methods of assessment and to the criteria being used by inspectors. Training is also necessary to analyse and interpret data accurately and to spot when they have been manipulated. Second, data leave out of consideration everything that cannot be measured – for instance, the morale, motivation, creativity and commitment of teachers and all those activities and facilities that enrich the quality of education – music, sport, libraries, dance, art and drama. The scope of inspection needs to be widened to encompass all that makes for a fulfilling education.

The government's desire to quantify a school's provision and to cut costs by outsourcing inspection to part-timers (some without educational qualifications) had, according to Pauline Perry, a former senior inspector for teacher training before Ofsted, dire consequences:

---

5   Tim Benson, a head of three different primary schools in East London, managed to find for the inspectors 'nine children who had been with us from start to finish; *nine* children – one per cent of our intake' (Benson, 2008: 3. Original emphasis).

... over the last 15 years the Ofsted inspector has become little more than a clerical officer ticking off pre-determined boxes of what should be judged, rather than a senior professional exercising professional judgement of the quality of pupils' learning.

(Perry, 2008: 50)

Ofsted has repeatedly changed its methods since then, but educators continue to claim that inspectors are arriving at schools with a pre-set agenda formed by consulting their test results and looking for evidence to support their expectations.

This case study has been discussed in some detail because it brings alive some of the main issues about inspection, but case studies must be treated with caution: they provide vivid illustration but they cannot be generalized. I shall give the last word to the head of the maths department who wished to signal 'the discrepancy between [Ofsted's] authoritative generalisations and the shakiness of the foundations upon which they are based'.[6]

2.3.2 The research evidence

The greater the consequences of favourable and unfavourable inspections, the greater the need for convincing evidence of their reliability and validity. Unfortunately there are no simple, unambiguous messages to be derived from the literature, which tends to be descriptive with few empirical studies. The findings from the first category tend to be personal accounts that are at times moving, but one cannot generalize from them. The findings from the second are either insightful and systematic, or inconclusive and trite. Good examples of both types of approach have been chosen and, as with the positive effects of inspection, three articles have been selected to examine in depth. The descriptive accounts will be summarized under the following headings: the impact of inspection on students, teachers and institutions; the stress caused by inspection; value for money; and self-evaluation and peer review.

Let me begin with Gray and Wilcox's proposition: 'Inspections are as good as their methodological foundations' (Gray and Wilcox, 1995: 127). If an inspection is unreliable or invalid or has precious little impact on the effectiveness of teaching, then the exercise is futile, a waste of taxpayers' money and potentially damaging. If parents, the government and the teaching profession are to have confidence in Ofsted, then each inspection should provide, at the very least, the following information:

---

6   Personal communication from the head of the maths department, 2014.

- a justification of the size and representativeness of the sample chosen for evaluation
- a measure of the reliability of the judgements made. How consistent are they?
- an assessment of the validity of the judgements made. Have the inspectors interpreted the data correctly?
- and, after six months, say, an account of the effects the inspection, both benign and undesirable.

When a school is closed teachers lose their jobs. The methods underpinning that judgement cannot be amateurish, they must observe these four basic standards. Just as the government insists on minimal thresholds of performance for attainment, then it is only right and proper for the Inspectorate to be held similarly to account. Further standards, such as the basic competencies needed in an inspector, will be discussed in the final chapter.

2.3.3 Empirical studies

2.3.3.1 Control group design

The gold standard of research in the medical sciences, of blind, randomized control groups, does not exist in education, as far as I know. The degree of control that can be attained in other fields is more difficult – what parents would want their children consigned to the control group while other people's children participate in an exciting new experiment? The nearest approach to the gold standard that I could find is a longitudinal, control-group design where schools in two German states were randomly selected from those chosen for inspection or from those awaiting their first inspection. This design was possible because inspections were introduced there for the first time in 2005/6. Another feature that makes this study an advance on cross-sectional evaluations is that teachers (and not just principals) were surveyed, although the mean response rate was only 21.7 per cent.

The results indicated that inspections 'have relatively little impact on the perception of school quality' (Gaertner *et al.*, 2014: 503), but there is an important caveat. In the two German states, inspection reports are not yet published and do not lead to serious consequences for schools. This underlines the importance of context and the specific political conditions within which inspection takes place. The results therefore cannot be transferred to this country, but they agree with other 'international research [which] casts doubt on the assumption that school inspection has largely positive effects' (Gaertner *et al.*, 2014: 491).

The evidence from countries like England and the Netherlands where the pressures from inspection and accountability create high risks for colleges comes to the same conclusion. Karen Jones and Peter Tymms, for example, summed up the current state of knowledge thus:

> At the moment there is a lack of evidence from strong research designs to assess the impact of inspections and the assumption that there is a causal link between inspections and school improvement cannot be clearly supported from the literature.
>
> (Jones and Tymms, 2014: 328)

That literature is replete with similar inconclusive findings principally because of the number and complexity of the intermediate factors between inspection and improvement. On to the second article.

2.3.3.2 UNDESIRABLE EFFECTS

In an overview of empirical studies which imposed order on a disorganized field, Inge de Wolf and Frans Janssens, who are simultaneously university-based researchers and members of the Netherlands' Inspectorate, draw a distinction between intended and undesirable effects of inspection, where the latter 'sometimes have the capacity to completely undo the intended effects' (de Wolf and Janssens, 2007: 382).

In the first category of 'intended strategic behaviour and gaming', the authors place: feedback influencing school policy; guaranteeing a minimum level of achievement; window dressing in order to be more favourably assessed; weaknesses concealed and staff aiming for a 'perfect week' (Ouston and Davies, 1998: 14); fraud or deception such as excluding weak students from tests[7]; or poor teachers absenting themselves to avoid inspection.

The second category of 'unintended strategic behaviour' includes: teaching to the test or teaching to inspection; an excessive emphasis on exam performance; a focus on short-term solutions at the expense of long-term improvement; reluctance to innovate; and teaching practices becoming similar across schools. Other side effects discussed are stress; good schools resting on their laurels; and public league tables stimulating market forces in education.

The article by de Wolf and Janssens provides a useful synthesis of a large number of empirical studies that include the finding that parents, when

---

7   A Dutch study found that about 30 per cent of schools were excluding pupils; see Altrichter and Kemethofer, 2014. This is also a growing problem in England as Warwick Mansell (2017) recently explained.

choosing schools, take little notice of performance indicators. I have two reservations. First, vague terms with Latin origins are used to describe simple behaviour. So, for example, focusing on records becomes 'formalization and proceduralization'; excluding pupils from exams becomes 'reshaping the test pool'; and reluctance to innovate becomes 'ossification'. Such language unintentionally reinforces the hierarchy where researchers and inspectors have the power to relabel the activities of teachers. Researchers have an obligation to present their findings to teachers, parents, students, policy-makers and politicians in language that is readily accessible to those who pay for their research; and the temptation to use pretentious, scientific sounding terms should be resisted.

The other reservation is the absence of any discussion of the example teachers are setting their pupils when they employ 'gaming' strategies. Students are aware of the intensive preparations and the explicit teaching of exam techniques, but they also witness the cheating deployed by their teachers. This can be seen as either detrimental to their moral development or ideal preparation for working in the gig economy.

2.3.3.3 EUROPEAN COMPARISONS

The third article is Frank Altrichter and David Kemethofer's survey of 2,300 principals of primary and secondary schools, in seven European countries, to investigate whether inspection promotes school improvement. From their comprehensive and insightful review of the literature, the researchers developed five hypotheses to test by sending out a questionnaire of 73 statements such as 'I feel pressure to do well on the inspection standards'. The replies were analysed by highly sophisticated statistical techniques that produced a set of trite conclusions such as 'school leaders who felt more "accountability pressure" say that more developmental activities take place in their schools' (Altrichter and Kemethofer, 2015: 50). Worryingly, those principals who experienced more pressure reported significantly more unintended consequences and admitted to discouraging new teaching methods and narrowing both the curriculum and instructional strategies.

The limitations of this research are openly admitted by the authors, but they form serious obstacles to its acceptance. For instance, as usual in such studies, only the subjective, self-reports of principals are sought, and classroom teachers, governors and students remain silent. The banal statements in the survey have all the appearance of having been concocted by a committee and the response rate in England was only 16 per cent in secondary and 13 per cent in primary schools. (In Ireland the corresponding percentages were 6 per cent and 4 per cent.) There is no mention of the cost of this research, but questions must be asked about the expense of sending out 1,422 questionnaires in England (and 3,200 in Ireland) for such meagre returns. The exclusive reliance on questionnaires and the absence of in-depth interviews reduce the value of this study that applied advanced statistical techniques to poor data.

2.3.4 Descriptive studies
2.3.4.1 IMPACT ON STUDENTS AND TEACHERS

These studies consist of accounts by senior managers and classroom teachers of their experiences of inspection, and what follows is an amalgam of them. They have little to say about the impact on students, although teachers mention their worries about the effects of coaching and spoon-feeding on their students' critical faculties, independence and understanding of the subjects they are studying. Some admit that the college's push for higher test results trumps their students' learning needs. As Carol Fitz-Gibbon put it: 'teachers are diverted from looking after pupils to looking after inspectors' (Fitz-Gibbon, 1998: 15). The charge here is that the pressures on educators to ratchet up test results year on year renders the learning of their students superficial, short-lived and, as I have called it elsewhere, bulimic (Coffield *et al.*, 2014). By that term I mean students binge on large amounts of information, spew it out in tests and then forget it. Learning is reduced to the skill of passing exams rather than the means of coming to understand and love their subjects.

Students have also become aware that their teachers need to focus their attention on those pupils who can enhance the school's test performance by gaining a C grade rather than a D. As one was overheard saying: 'If you want some help from the teacher, tell him you're a C/D borderline' (Fitz-Gibbon, 1998: 13). Those students comfortably above and those worryingly below this cut-off point consequently received less attention. The government has recently introduced two new accountability measures, called Progress 8 and Attainment 8, which seek 'to capture the progress a pupil makes from the end of primary school to the end of secondary school' (DfE, 2017: 5). The new system avoids the problems associated with the C/D borderline, but introduces others; for example, pupils' performance will now be compared with the national average rather than with performance of pupils from similar schools – good news for schools in affluent areas. To work effectively, this form of accountability is also heavily dependent on assessment at the end of primary school being accurate. The new measures are explained … in 42 pages.

The impacts of inspection on teachers both professionally and personally are no less serious. Some refer to the threats to their identities as teachers from having their work publicly denigrated; and this can happen to an 'outstanding' or 'good' teacher who has the misfortune to work in a school that is evaluated as 'failing' or 'requiring improvement'. Here, for instance, are the words of the staff of a school three months after an inspection that produced a good report and yet they 'still feel incensed by it. The feeling of impotency, rejection, depression and demoralisation it has left behind has no precedent in any other experience we have had' (Boothroyd and McNicholas, 1997: 15).

The recruitment and retention of teachers and senior managers are claimed to be adversely affected by Ofsted inspections, according to the former general secretary of the National Association of Headteachers. In his view, the ritual humiliation to which teachers in disadvantaged schools are repeatedly subjected, by the publication of league tables, is 'an inversion of social justice because they have the greatest challenges yet the least reward' (Brookes, 2008: 11). A headteacher with over 20 years of experience in tough schools in east London added that inspection 'helps to create a culture of fear in our most vulnerable schools: the very schools that need the most encouragement and support' (Benson, 2008: 32).

2.3.4.2 STRESS

Stress was reported at all stages of the inspection, from preparation through the process itself to the aftermath. Research found that many 'reported slowing down while they recovered from the "ordeal" of inspection – the "post-inspection blues"' (Ouston and Davies, 1998: 19). Some schools suffered from unusually high rates of absenteeism after inspection and some teachers suffered from 'severe stress, serious illness and sometimes the abandonment of a teaching career' (Fitz-Gibbon, 1996: 11). Headteachers noticed that it was often their most conscientious teachers who suffered most anxiety. Tutors in university departments of education were said, post-inspection, to feel a 'real sense of exhaustion, anger and disaffection' (Newby, 1998: 30). These feelings were explained in a letter Peter Tymms sent to the *Times Higher Education*. Each university department of initial teacher education was rated in 14 different areas. 'If it failed just one of them, it failed overall ... It must pick out four top, four good and eight "adequate" students ... if a single one of these is judged to be failing ... the institution fails' (Tymms, 1997).

Instead of quoting in full remarks from staff about inspection, I hope to convey the impression created by reading numerous such accounts from 1993 to 2017[8] by providing these snippets without comment: 'I was reduced to tears'; 'I was interrogated'; 'I've completely lost heart'; 'I'm so disillusioned I'm giving up teaching'; 'his comments were hurtful and humiliating'; 'it was a witch-hunt'; 'vultures circling round the school'; 'I had a nervous breakdown'; 'the experience was inhumane'; 'it took months to restore morale'; 'it was traumatic'; 'we were afraid of retribution if we complained'; 'it's harder to attract teachers now the school's been branded'; and 'improving takes longer than the period within which inspectors return'.[9]

The malaise was said to spread from the damage done to a school's reputation to its local community and that malaise could last for years. It can take generations of educators to build up the reputation of an FE college, but that reputation can be seriously damaged by Ofsted labelling it 'inadequate'. How can the complexity, dynamism and organic nature of a large FE college with, say, 15,000 students and 30 academic and vocational departments be reduced to one adjective? It is not statistically sensible to so label a large college, given the considerable variation from department to department, the 'snapshot' nature of inspection and the variation in student intake from year to year. If Ofsted were to make just one change, it must drop this overweening pretension to exactitude.

2.3.4.3 VALUE FOR MONEY

Ofsted's accounts show that its expenditure rose sharply from £63 million in 1993–4 to £200 million in 2010–11, but was cut back to £150 million in 2016–17 and is set to decline further to £127 million by 2019–20 (Ofsted, 2014: 8). Michael Power has calculated that the additional costs (of preparing for inspection, dry runs, etc.) double the direct costs. As these funds are diverted from schools and colleges, are we getting value for money? The issue is not whether there should be an inspectorate or not, but whether the current model of inspection is the most appropriate. David Hargreaves' question, posed in 1995, remains relevant: 'If it can be shown that other strategies are more effective *and* cost-effective, Ofsted's functions and priorities should be changed accordingly' (Hargreaves, 1995: 118). His article and subsequent publications went on to make a number of recommendations that I shall incorporate into my model. For the present,

---

8   These snippets have been extracted from emails sent to me, from the testimony of educators across the system at conferences, from newspaper and journal articles.

9   It could be argued that some stress is necessary to push the complacent into reform. Alexander the Great treated pain as just weakness leaving the body. The levels of stress recorded here, however, strike me as dysfunctional.

I leave the reader to decide if the evidence provided so far suggests that we are getting value for money.

2.3.4.4 Self-evaluation and peer review

The long and responsible tradition of self-evaluation in some English schools was largely superseded when Ofsted introduced the self-evaluation form (SEF) in an attempt to make inspections quicker and simpler, even though it issued guidance, encouraging schools to use their own methods. Within a short time, however, completing the SEF had become an industry, where senior managers attended workshops on how to complete it or employed private consultants to do it for them.

In the FE sector, colleges assessed their own activities and were then judged 'by a panel of peers from other high-performing colleges', but the process was complicated because 'a certain level of institutional maturity is needed in order to have the confidence to be able to identify and address the issues raised' (Earley, 1998: 175–6). The model of inspection used by the Further Education Funding Council (FEFC), which oversaw the work of FE and sixth-form colleges after they were removed in 1992 from the Local Education Authorities, contained many admirable features such as: the colleges were not assigned a single grade but all the main curriculum areas were assessed separately; dialogue between assessors and assessed was 'promoted by having a member of the college participate in the entire inspection process including meetings of the inspectors' (Fitz-Gibbon, 1993b: 2); and a full-time inspector was attached to each college before, during and after inspection to ensure that inspectorial knowledge was deep, accurate and constantly updated. The FEFC was abolished in 2000, the Adult Learning Inspectorate operated from then until 2007, when it in turn was taken over by Ofsted, whose methods prevailed – an example of Gresham's law where bad coinage drives out good.

Back in the schools, self-evaluation turned into self-regulation with headteachers becoming internal inspectors applying Ofsted's criteria; and inside every teacher there is now an inspector. John MacBeath commented: '… the more governments provide the frameworks, indicators and tools, the less inventive and spontaneous the process at school and classroom level' (MacBeath, 2008: 39). He went further by contrasting the characteristics of self-inspection with those of self-evaluation, which puts schools in charge of change rather than being controlled by it. His explanatory table is presented in Table 2.1.

Table 2.1: Self-inspection and self-evaluation

Self-inspection	Self-evaluation
Top down	Bottom up
A one-off event	Continuous and embedded in teachers' work
Provides a snapshot at a given time	A moving and evolving picture
Time consuming	Time saving
More about accountability than improvement	More about improvement than accountability
Applies a rigid framework	Flexible and spontaneous
Uses a set of predetermined criteria	Uses, adapts and creates relevant criteria
Creates resistance	Engages and involves people
Can detract from learning and teaching	Improves learning and teaching
Encourages playing safe	Takes risks

Source: MacBeath, 2008: 40

More recently, Challenge Partners, a co-operative cluster of 300+ primary, secondary and special schools, has developed a 'robust, independent, expertly led peer review system run by schools for schools that complements periodic inspection' (Matthews and Headon, 2015: 47). The essential conditions of success are given as: trust among equal partners that allows for reciprocal challenge; capable reviewers who are senior leaders from distant schools; and peer reviews adapted to the particular needs of the school.

There are many positive features of this approach that will be incorporated into my alternative model, but it has its weaknesses too, over and above the managerial cant about 'non-negotiables' and 'world class'. For example, the first aim of these peer reviews is to improve exam results as if that is all there is to education. The main outcome appears to be the professional development of senior leaders, but the independent evaluation has almost nothing to say about classroom teachers: the 'coal face' is mentioned as is the 'front line', but teachers do not merit a mention. What else would you expect from two ex-Ofsted inspectors, imbued with its philosophy that leadership is the most significant factor in improvement, who also believe that Ofsted represents 'the gold standard in evaluation expertise and quality criteria' (Matthews and Headon, 2015: xviii). The authors' shared background helps to explain why the claims for reliability of the process are weak and those for validity non-existent. These criticisms, however, do not detract from the wider significance of peer-led accountability – it is an essential building block in a self-improving system.

2.4 Summing up

Readers are likely to have formed strong opinions about Ofsted long before opening this book which, I hope, has demonstrated that the benefits and shortcomings of inspection are complex, contentious and constantly changing rather than clear-cut and conclusive. There should be at least general agreement with Campbell's law which predicted back in 1976 that the main unintended consequence of accountability will be to 'distort and corrupt the social processes it is intended to monitor' (Campbell, 1976: 49). Stefan Collini, writing about British universities, has provocatively added: 'what is most distinctive, and perhaps distinctively valuable, about what universities do is precisely what cannot be captured by the metrics societies increasingly use to measure value' (Collini, 2017a: 25). Substitute the word 'educators' for 'universities' in that sentence and it is still holds true.

Neither quotation should be taken to mean that there is no place for accountability in education. As Peter Drucker has argued, education has become much too important and much too expensive not to be held accountable (Drucker, 1994). The issue is rather what form accountability should take and my contention is that the balance of the evidence presented so far points firmly to the need for change and radical change at that. So my answer to the question posed in this chapter – does inspection do more harm than good? – is that the positive aspects of Ofsted's model need to be incorporated into a new approach that jettisons its damaging features.

The benefits of inspection can be briefly summarized as: monitoring the quality of education nationally, regionally and institutionally; reporting on general themes such as the quality of maths teaching; setting and raising expectations; providing feedback and then checking to see if it is acted on; involving key players such as parents, governors and the local community in the process; and its ability to challenge unquestioned assumptions, poor practices and incompetent teachers in order to stimulate improvement. These are important roles that must be retained.

On the other hand, empirical studies such as international surveys of inspection have concluded that the 'ultimate impact on student attainment is modest and indirect' (Ehren, 2014: 20). Added to that are the unintended consequences, the most serious of which are that educators are distracted from trying new curricula and teaching methods towards meeting the standards that Ofsted insist upon. That brings in its train all the demeaning attempts to 'game' the system. The descriptive studies of how educators have experienced inspection can be summed up in the phrase: inspection is felt as something done *to* them, not something done *with* them in the joint search for improvement.

Over the 24 years of its existence, Ofsted has acted as the enforcer of government policy and in so doing has been largely responsible for altering the culture of the teaching profession, changing the language and practices but not the values of educators. What was introduced in 1992 as an additional lever of change quickly became in the wrong hands a hammer that created a climate of fear and intimidation. The relationship between Ofsted and the teaching profession slipped into a downward spiral of recrimination on one side and resentment on the other. For me, the main criticism of Ofsted remains that its methods do not reflect what we now know about how learning best occurs, or how change can be best brought about in organizations and in systems. For who is inspired to learn by being publicly humiliated? Fear induces superficial compliance, defensiveness or rejection rather than learning. Surely we can improve education without so much angst and suffering. In Michael Power's words '… audit threatens to become a form of learned ignorance' (Power, 1997: 123).

The appointment of Amanda Spielman as CI, and her public declaration to reset the relationship between her organization and the teaching profession, to make it 'much more positive and purposeful', and to see her role as 'an enabling one … that gets the most from the valuable work' (Spielman, 2017: 2) of educators is most welcome. But the years of smouldering resentment at Ofsted and the low morale that it helped to create, will not be dispelled by a few well-intentioned speeches. That will take a new approach to inspection that creates educational growth for students, educators and inspectors. In the meantime, a little more humility from inspectors would be welcome. Instead of claiming to be 'doing good as we go' (Raeside, 2017: 1), Ofsted should adopt the motto 'we shall seek to do the minimum harm'. It is time for me to move from criticism to construction.

Part Two

A new model of inspection

Chapter 3

General principles to underpin the model

We need to move beyond the tyrannies of improvement, efficiency and standards, to recover a language of and for education articulated in terms of ethics, moral obligations and values.

(Ball, 2007: 191)

3.1 A legitimate and necessary role

There is general acceptance in the teaching profession that inspection plays a legitimate and necessary role in the accountability of a major public service like education. For some, accountability has become 'a largely negative instrument of social and political control [operating within] the culture and practice of blame' (Fielding, 2001: 699). The aim here is to recast accountability, to move it from an exclusive concentration on summative assessment (judging the more easily measurable outputs of education) towards a balance of both formative (improving the quality of TLA) and summative assessment.

The shift from the current model to one based on more educational principles will take time and will have to be fought for, as all the major players – government, inspectors, parents, governors and educators – must be convinced of its merits. What we cannot do is to continue with an approach that unintentionally encourages educators to improve their students' performance by excluding troublesome pupils; by concentrating on some students at the expense of others; and by using tactics that are nothing other than cheating, and which are the very antithesis of education. Accountability could still become the 'positive and practical tool' (Gilbert, 2012: 23) that the present system of hyper-accountability can never be.

We need a well-trained, knowledgeable, skilful and effective teaching profession whose work is evaluated by inspectors who have confidence in the methodology they are using because it is diverse, technically sound and has been negotiated with the inspected. Little will change, however, unless and until we re-establish between educators and inspectors a culture of mutual respect and the following five principles provide the moral basis to underpin that culture:

- education as growth
- restoring trust
- challenge matched by support
- dialogue
- appreciative inquiry.

3.2 Education as growth

Education is here treated as a process of productive growth for individuals, institutions, systems and society. Education helps us to shape our identities, to improve our performance as workers, parents and citizens, and it keeps active the brains of old-age pensioners like me. When we engage co-operatively together, education promotes the growth of social intelligence with which we can create the kind of society we want.[1] For John Dewey 'the value of school education is the extent in which it creates a desire for continued growth and supplies means for making the desire effective in fact' (Dewey, 1916: 53). So the most important attitude to form in students is the desire to go on learning – what has more recently been called lifelong learning.

What is the relevance of all this for Ofsted? It suggests that the first criterion of inspection should be: do students leave schools and colleges as lifelong learners who understand how to learn and who can assess their own weaknesses, strengths and enthusiasms as learners? Are the experiences of students in college educational (that is, do they lead to further productive growth)? Do some of their experiences stifle their curiosity and turn them against further learning? As a corollary, do our educators and inspectors have the resources, time and space to grow as professionals? Michael Fielding and Peter Moss sum up this first principle: 'Education is first and finally about how we learn to lead good lives together, lives that enable us individually and collectively to survive and flourish'. The new model of inspection must do nothing to diminish and everything to uphold this principle.

3.3 Restoring trust

> *It is only by talking about trust, and trusting, that trust can be created, maintained and restored.*
>
> (Solomon and Flores, quoted in Hargreaves, 2012: 15)

---

1   David Hargreaves quotes Chateaubriand: 'Les moments de crise produisent un redoublement de vie chez les hommes' – in Paul Auster's splendid translation: 'human beings don't begin to live fully until their backs are against the wall' (2004: 82).

Trust is '… the glue that binds together the network of schools involved in peer review and a key characteristic of their leadership.'

(Matthews and Headon, 2015: 3)

In education, the fear that has been the predominant force for change now needs to be replaced by trust. But how? The social relations between the Inspectorate and many educators have become embittered, but Ofsted's new policies, of recruiting inspectors from the leaders of institutions graded 'good' or 'outstanding' and of training them to become specialists in evaluation, will help to legitimate their authority. That authority now has to be earned and the task will be made easier if the chosen leaders are not all from schools with socially favoured intakes, where results are boosted by the work of private tutors.

Trust also requires, as Richard Sennett pointed out, a leap of faith in other people, 'not knowing whether that faith can be justified' (Sennett, 2012: 153). If, however, the inspectorate were to generously endorse the view that the prevailing ethos of educators 'is both to want, and to do, good work' (Sennett, 2012: 170), then that public recognition would help to counteract the decades of mistrust that has built up between the two groups. Mutual respect will also grow when teachers learn the skills of evaluation from inspectors, who in turn loudly sing the praises of those committed educators in FE who help students damaged by repeated failure at school become resourceful and confident learners. Inspectors also need to assess the extent to which they are being successful in transmitting their skills in evaluation to educators; in this way they could ensure that the processes of self-evaluation are being embedded by practitioners and institutions.

Nor should the relationship between inspectors and educators be soured by the small minority of incompetent teachers. Every sizeable profession has members who prove not to be up to the job and who need to be removed firmly and respectfully, but the much bigger problem is those experienced teachers who need support to become expert teachers. John Hattie and Gregory Yates have summarized the research into the attributes of expert teachers who, far more than experienced teachers, have the interpersonal sensitivity to diagnose where students are in their learning, have a battery of interventions to call on and routinely evaluate the impact of their intervention on students' learning (Hattie and Yates, 2014: 103–10).

David Hargreaves has done more than most to show how school leaders 'must model trust, audit and build it' (Hargreaves, 2012: 13). He devised tests to audit how much trust staff have in their headteacher, how much staff have in one another and how much students have in the staff. It would be a simple matter to devise a further test of how much trust classroom teachers and managers have in the inspectorate. We will know that trust has been restored when educators report that inspection is now done *with* them and not *to* them. There is also a simple way of testing how much trust senior leaders have in their staff: are they trusted to work at home when not timetabled to work in school or college? Conversations in staffrooms about TLA and particular students can only take place, however, if teachers are present.

3.4 Challenge matched by support

The performance of students in exams and of educational institutions during inspection may differ significantly from their underlying capability. Exams and inspection provide limited data on which to base a judgement on whether capability has been accurately assessed. Inspectors are also aware that educators are likely to be more guarded and less willing to reveal weaknesses or to open their standard practices for evaluation, than when they are being reviewed by their peers. All the more reason for the basis of inspection to shift from a heavy emphasis on challenge to one where challenge is carefully balanced by an equal concern for supporting schools in those areas that need attention.

Inspectors must still be free to question the way in which the school defines its strengths and weaknesses. Inspection 'has to be a challenging process, not a question of superficially testing and rubber-stamping the school's view of itself' (Matthews and Headon, 2015: 44). Unwelcome news is more likely to be accepted and acted on, however, if it is accompanied by explicit offers of support to address, for instance, blind spots, or to access expertise in teaching physics, say, or to collaborate on admitted weaknesses. This will require Ofsted to promote and foster a culture of collaboration.

There are good educational reasons and research to back this principle. Jean Piaget, for example, was in favour of teachers deliberately creating disequilibrium in the minds of their students, but only as part of the continual search for a higher and better equilibrium. Similarly, Jerome Bruner argued that 'the art of raising challenging questions is easily as important as the art of giving clear answers ... Good questions are ones that pose dilemmas, subvert obvious or canonical "truths", force incongruities upon our attention' (Bruner, 1996: 127).

What types of support should inspectors be offering the inspected? Continuity of concern could be established by attaching an inspector to a college before, during and after the inspection to ensure that the college is fully understood and that its responses to the plan of action (developed and agreed between senior managers and the inspection team) are monitored. Inspectors also need to assess how much help a school needs to implement the agreed recommendations and to communicate this assessment to the staff, governors and parents. They would transform the relationship with teachers, however, if the inspectors stayed in the school for, say, a month to work with the staff on implementing the action plan. Schools may also identify particular forms of expertise that they need to strengthen, for example, in dealing with dyslexia, and the inspectorate could suggest schools where TLA in those areas are exemplary. Inspectors are also well placed to suggest where educators' colleagues in other institutions have successfully incorporated Joint Practice Development (JPD) as their major form of staff development. JPD is proving to be a major advance in professional learning over teachers 'sharing practice', which may not change what they do in classrooms; instead they jointly (J) evaluate their practice (P) in order to develop it (D) (Fielding *et al.*, 2005; Hargreaves, 2012).

3.5 Dialogue

> *Dialogue is the antithesis of a state theory of learning, and its antidote.*
>
> (Alexander, 2010: 307)

When Ofsted conducted a survey of school leaders' views on the impact of inspection, a key finding was that the most useful aspect of inspection was thought to be dialogue during the inspection – more helpful than the analysis of strengths and weaknesses or feedback to senior staff or the recommendations for improvement. Dialogue with the lead inspector helped school leaders to understand the 'reasons and evidence behind the judgements' (Ofsted, 2015a: 12).

If the purpose of this dialogue is professional learning for educators and inspectors, then it must go beyond comfortable conversation to allow for 'challenge and disagreement as well as consensus' (Alexander, 2006: 24). To ensure that the interactions between inspectors and educators involve a productive exchange of ideas and possibilities, their dialogue could be guided by the five criteria that Robin Alexander proposed for classrooms and that have been amended to fit the present context.

The learning of both parties will be enhanced if their dialogue is:

* *Collective* – inspectors and educators tackle problems together

- *Reciprocal* – educators and inspectors actively listen to each other, share ideas and consider alternative interpretations of data
- *Supportive* – educators articulate their ideas and concerns freely without fear of retribution
- *Cumulative* – inspectors and educators build on their own and each other's ideas and develop them into coherent lines of enquiry and improvement
- *Purposeful* – educators and inspectors plan for their dialogue with specific educational goals in mind.

(Alexander, 2006: 38, amended Coffield)

In these ways, dialogue, free from constraint, becomes central to expanding the possibilities for improvement.

3.6 Appreciative inquiry (AI)

… through our assumptions and choice of method we largely create the world we later discover.

(Cooperrider and Srivastva, 1987: 129)

Appreciative Inquiry (AI) is an approach to organizational change that pulls together the four principles already discussed – education as growth, restoring trust, challenge matched by support and dialogue – and then adds something distinctive of its own. The fundamental ideas were enunciated by David Cooperrider and Suresh Srivastva in 1987 and have been applied to educational (as well as business) contexts ever since. AI builds on the strengths of a school rather than seeking to minimize its weaknesses; it makes a conscious choice to study the best of a college, what it calls its 'positive core'; and it is neither a top-down nor a bottom-up process, but rather a 'whole system' approach. The methods used to intervene in the life of a school are epitomized by the '4-D Cycle', which begins with *Discovery* (appreciating the best of what is), then moves on to *Dream* (imagining the future), next is *Design* (building together what might be), and finally *Destiny* (empowering everyone to create the desired future).

If Ofsted were to adopt the methods of Appreciate Inquiry, inspectors, teachers and students would jointly negotiate an improvement plan; together they would generate internally the knowledge of how to bring those improvements about and the responsibility and initiative would be shared with educators to ensure the improvements were implemented.

AI enthusiasts are fond of drawing an unfavourable comparison between their perspective and problem solving where, for instance, the inspectors focus on the school's weaknesses and the headteacher 'arrives at the meeting with an arsenal of defences designed to protect his or her hard-won self-esteem' (ibid.; 139). For Cooperrider and Srivastva, 'problem solving tends to be inherently conservative [because] by definition, a problem implies that one already has knowledge of what "should be"' (ibid.: 147). In contrast AI shifts the blame away from individuals towards improving systems. Experienced practitioners of AI concede that three parts of AI are needed for every one part of problem solving: clearly both approaches are required.

Overviews have examined the transformational outcomes claimed for AI when it has been used in education, health, small private firms and large international corporations. Gervase Bushe and Aniq Kassam, for instance, studied twenty cases where AI had been applied and concluded that two qualities of the approach were key to transformative change. First was 'a focus on changing how people think instead of what they do' (Bushe and Kassam, 2005: 161). In the successful cases, the teachers generated new knowledge among themselves and this provoked new actions. This finding is completely at variance with the results of studies into an effective form of staff development called JPD, where the emphasis is on exactly the opposite, namely where teachers together improve what they do in classrooms and not just what they know (Hargreaves, 2011: 10) – a case where research could usefully be employed to explore the conflict.

The second quality was named 'improvised planned change', where management stopped prescribing or controlling teachers' efforts at change and instead nurtured the improvisations that flowed from the new ideas they had created. The authors also confirmed that asking about both strengths and weaknesses led to a fuller inquiry than just focusing on the former.

Examples of the successful adoption of Appreciative Inquiry in English schools are available; for example, the evaluation of a research project to help pupils make a more successful transition from primary to secondary school (Lift Off, 2016). The formative approach of AI allowed effective and ineffective practices to be studied in a way that secured the engagement, and motivation to change, of both pupils and teachers. The techniques employed by the researchers in this case could just as easily be used by inspectors.

I react badly, however, to anyone writing about the 4 Ds, the 5 Cs or the 6 Ps, by means of which many business gurus attempt to impose simplicity upon the messy peculiarities of organizations. There is also a strain in the AI literature that reads as if a disciple has stumbled across a new creed where 'visionary leaders … facilitate change at a rate that is unprecedented … in less than three days' (Stratton-Berkessel, 2015: 9). Asking educators to perform transformational change presents a formidable challenge, but miraculous change is beyond us all. Small but significant steps in the right direction can, however, be made by building on what is already a strength which is the main thrust of the AI approach. We can also invite colleagues to present to the inspectorate a united and collegial front, even if it hurts to do so.

Chapter 4

Main components of the alternative model

Anyone caught referring to citizens, passengers, students and others as 'customers' will be subject to an on-the-spot fine. We shall abolish the word 'incentivise'.

(Collini, 2017b: 3)

4.1 Introduction

My new model of inspection has nine interacting parts that make up a pragmatic, collaborative, formative and open-ended system that promotes the learning of all those associated with it. Each main theme will be briefly described, together with a set of attendant questions currently unasked by Ofsted, which are meant to be innovative, incisive and exacting – the adjectives 'robust' and 'rigorous' will be avoided, as official texts have, through overuse, rubbed them smooth of meaning. There is no suggestion that all of these questions should be asked on all occasions; rather, they should be used as a bank where withdrawals are made to suit the context. The questions could assume a life of their own by being used not just for inspection but as prompts for staff development. The model in its current form is an imperfect and incomplete sketch rather than a fully worked-out blueprint, so I repeat the invitation to readers, to contact me about any omissions, incoherence or impracticalities, at f.coffield@ucl.ac.uk

4.2 Teaching, Learning and Assessment: The first priority

The number one priority in education is Teaching, Learning and Assessment (TLA), which should be treated as one interacting system and not as three separate processes. So, it would not be wise to have a policy document on teaching and learning and a separate one on assessment because the blow-back from the current heavy-handed and poorly conceived form of assessment distorts both what students are taught and how they are taught it; and yet many colleges continue to have separate policies. Nor is education the simple sum of T + L + A. The challenges and the excitements of education lie in the unpredictable interactions between tutors and students; it is more like T x L x A.

Questions about students: The questions asked in Chapter 3.2 about whether students leave college as lifelong learners will not be repeated here but they are of prime importance. In addition, we could ask: do they appreciate that assessment is one of their best hopes for intellectual growth? Do they act on the feedback they receive? What do they think of the quality of that feedback? Are they aware that being shown what they need to know next is more important than the grades they receive? Can they assess their own work? Are they learning the skills of assessment from their teachers? What do they learn from working alongside and assessing fellow students? What learning strategies do they use and how effective are they? Most of these questions are drawn from the work of Paul Black and Dylan Wiliam, who introduced the idea of Assessment *for* Learning (AfL) (Black and Wiliam, 2009; Wiliam, 2011). AfL, however, as Dylan Wiliam now acknowledges, is not so much about assessment as about improving the quality of teaching.

Questions about educators: Do they have explicit theories of learning and how do they use these to evaluate and enhance their teaching? Do newly qualified teachers of, say, maths, realize that 'the task of learning how to teach maths successfully is every bit as difficult as learning maths in the first place'?[1] Are the different capabilities of students accounted for in their teaching? How varied are the teaching methods they use? Is the whole curriculum covered? Are able students stretched, especially those from disadvantaged backgrounds? What strategies are being used to close the gap between low and high-achieving students? Do teachers explain explicitly to students not only what constitutes good and excellent work in their subject, but also how they can progress in skills, knowledge and understanding from, say, GCSE to AS level and on to A2 level? What evidence is there of improvement? Are educators aware of what they teach well and how students respond? What aspects of their teaching make learning more difficult for students? Do staff and students jointly study aspects of TLA in order to improve them? Does the feedback given to students change their thinking or behaviour? If it does not, it is not feedback.[2] Do tutors make their students fall in love with questioning everything?

Questions about senior managers: Are they experts in TLA and how to encourage such knowledge in colleagues? Do they provide staff with the dedicated time, resources and space to learn? Do they know who are their expert teachers and have they strategies for such experts to work across a

---

1   Richard Noss, personal communication, 2017.
2   See Coffield *et al.*, 2014, Chapter 8, 'Harnessing the potential power of feedback'.

partnership? What explicit theories do leaders hold about TLA? Do they know how implicit theories can be made explicit? What are the merits and limitations of these theories? What support mechanisms are there for nurturing mediocre teachers who could with help become far more effective? What strategies are there for dismissing with dignity incompetent teachers? Do senior staff exemplify their stated belief in the pre-eminence of TLA by actually doing some teaching?

4.3 Professional Learning: The engine of improvement

Not the least reason why educators should be continually developing their skills and knowledge is that they need the professional confidence to challenge the assumptions, methods and findings of the inspectorate.

Questions about educators: Is their Professional Learning (PL) focused on improving students' learning? Is it part of a sustained, coherent programme over which they have control or is the programme decided by management? Does their chosen programme of PL dovetail with the learning needs of their students and of their institution? Do they learn collaboratively, with colleagues in school-based, peer-to-peer activities such as JPD? (Fielding *et al.*, 2005; Hargreaves, 2012: 8–12) Are they improving their subject knowledge and the best ways of teaching it? Can they admit to gaps in knowledge and weaknesses in teaching and have them addressed? What evidence do they use to assess the impact of their teaching? Do they welcome being engaged in challenging but constructive dialogue with inspectors? Do they have the time to put new ideas into practice?

Questions about senior managers: If Professional Learning is the major engine of school improvement, what percentage of the budget is spent on PL and how could it be increased? Is the culture of the college as conducive to the learning of tutors as it is to the learning of students? What model of staff development do they have and how effective is it? Do they participate fully in training days or are 'administratrivia' used as an excuse for non-attendance? Is the impact of PL evaluated by examining both quantitative and qualitative data on the quality of provision, teaching methods and student learning? Are staff/student ratios worsening? Do workloads enable staff to have a full personal life that allows them to grow as people? Is trust monitored, audited and enhanced? Is the notion of 'leadership' examined in PL?

4.4 Democracy: *The* fundamental British value

… schools are allegedly a preparation for participation in a democracy but are run in ways which apply rules and sanctions to children which would not be acceptable to adults.

(Stephen Ball, 2017: 82)

The vote in June 2016 to leave the European Union provoked a debate about British values; there are three that I think receive less attention than they deserve. First, do not rock the boat even if the captain is driving it into the cliffs. Second, a preference for amateurs over professionals that amounts to an anti-intellectualism that was evidenced in Michael Gove's claim that 'the British people have had enough of experts'. Third, the beliefs, more neoliberal than purely British, that business leaders – without any training – can run hospitals, FE colleges and prisons better than specialists who have spent their professional lives learning the complexities of the job.

Most commentators agreed, however, that *the* British value is democracy and the argument is backed up by reference to, for instance, the Magna Carta, the mother of parliaments and the war against fascism. To prevent extremism and to challenge intolerance in education, the coalition government launched in 2011 the Prevent Strategy that defined 'fundamental British values' as 'democracy, the rule of law, individual liberty and mutual respect and tolerance of different faiths and beliefs' (DfE, 2013: 9). The job of inspecting these values was then passed to Ofsted.

Is inspection, however, improving the health of democracy in schools, colleges and local communities? This recent governmental concern for democracy was a reaction to the fear of fundamentalist values and radicalization spreading in schools. It is a weak and limited definition of democracy, which has nothing to say about introducing democracy into national or local decision-making or into how schools, colleges or universities are run; and they are at present run undemocratically. Stefan Collini argues that education 'is in one sense irreducibly democratic – the best arguments and the best evidence are decisive, no matter who puts them forward' (Collini, 2017a: 27). That is true when the issue is winning an argument, but in an enfeebled democracy like ours the best argument and the most convincing evidence are frequently spurned when political decisions are made.

What would happen if those who had shared responsibility for a school were asked what they would like it to be judged on? Michael Fielding and John Elliott invited the governors, parents, community members, teachers and students in a college in Essex to construct a set of quality criteria by which it wished to be judged internally and externally (Fielding *et al.*, 2006). The criteria they democratically agreed upon differ significantly from those used by Ofsted and consisted of: parent–teacher relationships; teacher–student relationships; the intra-school organization into three smaller schools; curriculum and teaching; engaging and motivating students; discipline; and, last of all, assessment. Some aspects of this approach could be adopted by Ofsted, for example, by using Appreciative Inquiry to ask the local community responsible for a school: what makes this a good school? What is it proud of? What are its core values and aspirations? And what would it like to be judged on? What this community thought most important of all was the quality of teachers' relationships with parents and with students.

Questions: Do students experience democratic ways of working? Are they engaged in the social and political life of their communities? Where would the institution be placed, according to Michael Fielding's six levels of deepening participation of students in their education? (Fielding, 2016). Students at the first level are treated as a source of data about their satisfaction, collected by an annual survey. (One might expect feedback from students to improve the quality of teaching, but the way the mechanism was being used, as reported by a group of young economic graduates, created 'a culture of passivity and disengagement' (Earle *et al.*, 2017: 135), partly because the data was collected from final year students who would have left the university before any changes could take place.) The sixth level of democratic participation has been reached when educators and students are living, learning and working harmoniously and productively within a fully democratic institution.

The questions that arise from this approach are: Do tutors involve students in dialogue about, say, improving TLA? Do educators and students act like partners in learning by jointly evaluating, say, a curriculum unit? Are students equipped to carry out a study into an issue of concern to them such as low-level disruption in class? Do students and staff work collaboratively together to plan, say, a week's teaching? How and by whom are key issues that affect students' experiences of education decided?

FE colleges have led the way in listening and responding to the voices of their students and of local employers, but there are other voices that deserve to be heard: the voices of tutors. Politicians are convinced of the efficacy of student voices in improving TLA, yet they remain deaf to the voices of those who have the most power to enhance the quality of TLA: educators. I recently presented an equivalent ladder of increasing participation by tutors, again with six levels, which suggests the following questions: are tutors' views anonymously gathered and their concerns addressed? (Coffield, 2016). Do senior managers involve tutors in dialogue about, say, improving TLA? Do educators act as partners with senior managers to produce college policies? Is JPD used to enhance not only the practice of classroom teachers but also that of managers? Do management and tutors operate in Professional Learning communities to decide on the main issues facing the college? Finally, are those institutions striving to become learning communities (the characteristics of which will be described under section 4.6) treated as respected partners in a democratic education system, where they are regularly consulted about proposed policy changes and where they feedback to government their evaluation of policies they have enacted?

4.5 What curriculum do students need?

> As for school itself, that experience had driven my parents out of the education system and denied them access to culture … culture, the education system, books had all given us a feeling of rejection: in return we rejected them.
>
> (Édouard Louis, 2017)

If the curriculum does not respect and incorporate the culture, concerns and language of the students, then those students are likely to turn against it, the school and education more generally – and who can blame them? All curricula are selections from the various forms of knowledge such as science and the humanities and as such are not politically or socially neutral. The so-called 'national' curriculum was never compulsory for private schools and does not have to be followed by 'free' schools or academies. The English Baccalaureate closely resembles the grammar school curriculum of the 1950s and will still be relevant if it provides students with the knowledge, skills and understanding needed to tackle the main threats to our collective well-being, such as: climate change; widening inequalities and financial crises; an economy overly dependent on financial services to the disadvantage of manufacture; an ageing population without adequate provision for care; underfunded public services; obesity, and so on.

It will be argued that the content of the curriculum is under the control of the government rather than of Ofsted. Agreed. The Inspectorate, however, has the responsibility to report to the Secretary of State for Education on the state of education in England's schools and colleges. What an irony it would be if every year thousands of institutions are inspected and millions of pounds of taxpayers' money are spent, but the issue of whether students are receiving a curriculum relevant to their needs and future lives is not even mentioned.

Questions: Does the present curriculum prepare students to overcome these threats collaboratively? Are they involved in tackling together real problems where they discuss, research and share ideas in order to produce new ways of responding appropriately? As well as decontextualized subject knowledge, are the culture and concerns of the local community dealt with so that students can both recognize themselves and transcend their origins? Does the curriculum provide students with the capacity to think critically and the courage to think differently? Are students encouraged and given the necessary abilities to develop their own curricula on what concerns them most?

For those who find that notion too radical, the experimental education of pre-school children in Reggio Emilia in Italy (Fielding and Moss, 2011) and the new approach to the curriculum of economics, developed by a group of dissenting graduate students (Earle *et al.*, 2017: 2 and 5), show persuasively how critical and creative people of all ages can be. The students' determination to rethink economics stemmed from frustration 'with how little our education was helping us understand the world', their 'shared feeling that there was a deep malaise at the heart of economics', and their desire 'to democratise economics because we believe that at its core economics should be a public discussion about how to organise society' (ibid.). Substitute the word 'inspection' for 'economics' and 'education' for 'society' and the purposes of this book are restated in this quotation.

4.6 From exam factories to learning communities

We will know we have created learning communities in education when innovative teams of educators have the freedom, time and resources to take risks, fail and so improve; when the creativity of every student and member of staff – academic, vocational and support – has been released; when inspection covers all that schools offer and not just test and exam results; and when inspectors, managers, classroom teachers and students confidently discuss what theories of learning they espouse and how they use them to evaluate and enhance their learning. Readers who wish for a comprehensive introduction to learning communities are referred to the many useful sources of research and development (Watkins, 2005; Stoll and Louis, 2007; Timperley, 2011; Crowley, 2014; Coffield *et al.*, 2014). Here the concern is to treat a learning community as more than a group of like-minded people with productive, interpersonal relationships, but educators with shared, democratic values, ways of working and goals, who communicate honestly and sensitively with colleagues inside and outside of their institution and who enjoy working and learning together to improve students' learning.

Questions: Is learning the central organizing principle of the college? If not, what is? Is principled dissent well received, if not positively encouraged, as a means of finding alternative and more effective practices? Is the college the thriving hub of its community? Does Ofsted have an agreed theory or theories of learning and how it improves the practice of inspectors? Are students and educators part of different dynamic, creative teams that cut across disciplinary and subject boundaries in the search for innovative solutions? How are new ideas tested before they are incorporated in standard practices? Are the challenges presented to the inspected matched by adequate levels of support?

4.7 Resources: The elephant missing from the room

The new national funding formula for schools announced in December 2016 provoked an aggressive response from headteachers who sent letters to parents claiming that school funding was in crisis, and some heads requested regular donations of up to £600 per year (Adams, 2017). This is not the place to explore this issue except to say that it makes the obvious point that the level of resource has an immediate effect on the quality of provision. The failure to include any mention of the resources available to the institution under inspection is a case of the elephant missing from the room. Without detailed information on the funding available, the superior performance of an 'outstanding' school could be the result of a higher than average complement of teachers who are receiving a richer form of professional learning, while at the same time teaching smaller groups of students who have been vetted to exclude those with learning difficulties. So, in the new model, the level of resource will be an essential part of the data collected by inspectors.

While school leaders are reacting badly to a proposed cut of 6.5 per cent in real terms by 2019–20, the media are silent about the spending per FE student having decreased by 6.7 per cent since 2010 with a further drop of 6.5 per cent planned by 2019–20, which will reduce funding for 16–18 year olds to the level of 1988 (Belfield *et al.*, 2017). Is it not part of the duty of inspectors to highlight these glaring inequalities in their reports?

Questions: How do the institution's resources compare locally, regionally and nationally? Are the budget, staffing levels, library, buildings, technology, and resources for the arts and physical education adequate?

What percentages of supply/agency, untrained and newly qualified staff are there? What percentage of vocational tutors have recent and relevant experience of their specialism? What size are classes? Unit costs? Average weekly teaching load? What workload pressures (for example, administrative tasks) do educators consider unnecessary? What percentage of senior and middle managers do not teach? Are senior managers able to plan with a degree of certainty for the medium and long term?

4.8 Context: Not a backdrop but an active force

The context of institutions is taken into account in inspections, but it tends to be treated as 'just a backdrop against which schools have to operate' (Ball *et al.*, 2012: 24) rather than as an active force in its own right. Stephen Ball and his colleagues have differentiated four dynamic aspects of context that interact and overlap with each other:

- location – the catchment area, intake and history of the institution
- professional cultures – the management style, values, language, practices, personalities and commitment of staff, student-centred TLA, the number of new, part-time and agency staff
- physical/material – budget, buildings, facilities, infrastructure, IT support
- external – position in league tables, high parental expectations of academic success, Ofsted reports, governmental changes to curriculum and assessment, local competitors, local labour markets.

Each institution will present a particular and sometimes unexpected set of opportunities and constraints. For instance, pupils from impoverished homes may still arrive in secondary schools as confident and competent learners with a wide range of learning strategies, provided they have been taught these abilities in primary schools (Rose *et al.*, 2016). Again, parents with high aspirations for their children may encourage senior managers to focus narrowly on exam results at the expense of teaching students critical thinking skills (Tan, 2016). So a more dynamic and holistic understanding of context needs to be included in the reformed model of inspection.

Local context is likely to become increasingly important because partnerships are more likely to be formed among schools and colleges in the same area, which can tap into the same local networks to form programmes of mutual support, appropriate to their history, geography and culture.

Questions: What is the unique combination of constraints and opportunities in this institution and how do they interact? What allowances are made for these in inspection? What is the structure of local opportunities?

What is the quality of induction programmes, the tutorial system, careers guidance, work experience, apprenticeships and the first jobs of former students? What access, participation and achievement are available to groups traditionally under-represented in education? Can newcomers to education find places in the economic, cultural, social and political life of the community? Are resources sufficient to meet the requirements of equal opportunities and students with disabilities?

Has Ofsted developed different criteria to judge those tough schools serving areas of social deprivation, poor housing and high unemployment, which suffer from chronic recruitment difficulties, high student mobility and yet are committed to educating some students who are 'learning in their third or fourth language'? (Benson, 2008: 27). It would be clearly unjust if such schools' exam performance were to be compared to national averages. At present, those who have chosen to work in the most challenging of schools and colleges claim that Ofsted is not taking sufficient account of adverse local circumstances and so making a very demanding job almost impossible.[3] That cannot be a perverse outcome of inspection that is just accepted by those working in more comfortable environments.

4.9 Self-improving inspection to support a self-improving system

Ofsted's role, according to some commentators[4] should be restricted to reporting to Parliament on the quality of England's schools and colleges. That would make the Chief Inspector's (CI) Annual Report rather expensive at £150 million a year. It would also be a waste of 30 years of accumulated expertise in evaluation. Making Ofsted a force for improvement, as the new CI, Amanda Spielman, announced, reinforces the original purpose of the organization which was 'to make a contribution ... to raising standards and improving the quality of educational experience and provision' (Ofsted, 1994).

An overarching concern for improvement brings together all the earlier components of this alternative model, as set out in sections 4.2 to 4.8. The primary responsibility for improvement, however, was transferred from government to the teaching profession by the new coalition administration in 2010 that aimed 'to create a school system which is more effectively self-improving' (DfE, 2010: 73). This 'power shift to the front line'[5] is supported by increased numbers of National and Local Leaders of Education, and

---

3   For example, Tim Benson, 2008.
4   For example, Geraint Jones, 2017.
5   See David Hargreaves, 2012.

Teaching Schools; it is also visible in the intriguing variety of partnerships, networks, federations, multi-academy trusts, chains and family clusters that have evolved since then. This has become such a significant change that partnership (the term used to stand in for all these approaches) merits becoming the ninth dimension in the new model.

The most elegant and original model of what a mature self-improving school system should look like was drawn up by David Hargreaves. It consists of three main dimensions (each with four strands which are listed in the footnote): professional learning, the competence to develop partnerships, and the collective capacity for collaboration in the interests of improvement.[6] His persuasive narrative has been followed widely in England and Australia; my interest here is to envisage what should be the consequent changes for Ofsted.

According to the then Prime Minister, David Cameron, and the then Deputy Prime Minister, Nick Clegg, who wrote in 2010 a joint preface to the report *The Importance of Teaching*, devolving power to schools 'needs to be accompanied by a streamlined and effective accountability system' (DfE, 2010: 4), in which the performance measures used to hold schools to account were to be strengthened still further. This is the typical approach of senior politicians: they devolve power with one hand while steadily increasing their control from the centre with the other. An alternative future is worth considering. As the new inter-school partnerships become standard practice and take responsibility for the evolution of a self-improving system, the need for Ofsted diminishes and it slowly fades away. Or perhaps not.

There will remain the following functions for a reformed Ofsted to perform, even when a fully self-improving system is in place:

- Independent, external evaluation to monitor the performance of all educational institutions, but conducted with the different principles, themes and questions detailed earlier. One inspection every three or four years. This role is retained to prevent any backward slippage into cosy complacency in self-evaluations or peer reviews.

---

6   The bare bones of the model are:

    a)   Professional Development: joint practice development, mentoring and coaching, talent identification and distributed staff information

    b)   Partnership Competence: fit governance, high social capital, collective moral purpose and evaluation and challenge

    c)   Collaborative Capital: analytical investigation, disciplined innovation, creative entrepreneurship and alliance architecture. For a full account see David Hargreaves, 2012.

- A concentration on schools serving tough areas – the terms 'failing', 'inadequate' and 'requiring improvement' will be dropped.
- Monitoring the building, maintenance (and occasional termination) of partnerships; liaising with the more frequent (annual?) peer reviews conducted by schools themselves. A balance of external and internal evaluations makes good sense.
- Conducting thematic reviews across institutions; for example, how best to close the gap between under-performing and high-achieving students; or how to improve the literacy and numeracy of students who have failed GCSE exams in these two all-important subjects.
- Ensuring that Ofsted matches self-improving schools by itself becoming self-improving, by means of research and development into its assumptions, training, methods and practices; by disseminating the skills of evaluation throughout the teaching profession; and by Ofsted inspectors becoming the acknowledged experts in evaluation.

Questions about educators: What benefits from the partnership are gained by: students, educators, middle and senior managers, the education system? Is mutual challenge among partnership schools matched by mutual support? How have staff responded to being made responsible for the success of the students in partner schools as well as in their own? How is co-operation to work alongside competition, especially in those areas where new grammar schools are set up? Is there a healthy balance between competition and collaboration? How well-developed are the diagnostic skills of staff when assessing the strengths and weaknesses of their partners? Are students and classroom teachers leading the search for innovative solutions? How manageable are the innovations they come up with? What are students and staff learning about the processes of innovation and how it should be disseminated across the partnership? What are the main achievements and unfinished business of the partnership?

Questions for inspectors: What changes are needed to the current model of inspection to ensure it supports a self-improving system? What do inspectors need to learn about the building and maintenance of partnerships? For example, what stage has the partnership reached – beginning, developing, embedded or leading?[7] Is the partnership becoming so big it is in danger of becoming a monopoly? How big can multi-academy trusts become and still be successful? How deep do the links go below senior management? Do partnerships direct attention towards senior and middle management

---

7   These terms are taken from David Hargreaves, 2011: 9.

and away from those on whom success mainly depends, namely classroom teachers? What joint activities are truly collaborative? What are the costs to the partnership in time, resources and other opportunities foregone? Do the benefits clearly outweigh the costs? Are the arrangements for the governance of the partnership appropriate? How soon can inspectors detect that a partnership has become complacent or is drifting or has become dysfunctional? What support can Ofsted organize for those schools facing the toughest challenges? What current assumptions and practices of Ofsted need to change? What plans do Ofsted have for disseminating the skills of evaluation among practising teachers?

4.10 Obstacles to a self-improving system

The emergence of a self-improving system is likely to encounter some obstacles and the most obvious deserve a moment's discussion. First, are educators prepared to share their craft knowledge to benefit all students and not just those in the schools where they teach? Time will tell, but my experience would indicate that those educators who make careers within the profession do so for altruistic reasons and so would be most likely to extend their commitment to all students with little if any resistance.

Second, there is a disconnection between the levels of satisfaction with inspection reported by Ofsted and those related to more independent researchers. The disparity can be addressed by regular, independent monitoring of the trust that the teaching profession has in Ofsted, but the deeper issue is whether the Inspectorate – and government ministers – can learn to trust the judgement of educators. As self-evaluation and peer review become ever more established and uncontroversial features of the system, the growing culture of trust should encourage Ofsted to rely more on the professionalism of educators, especially with regard to assessment, external as well as internal. This could open the door to a re-evaluation of government's dogmatic obsession with exam results as the principal, if not the sole, means of judging quality in education. The education system will be reaching maturity when Ofsted inspectors and educators (not just senior managers) engage in open and genuine dialogue, where the former realize they have much to learn from the latter about TLA and the latter much to learn about evaluation from the former. As trust between the two parties deepens, they could start challenging each other's most cherished assumptions with the aim of improving the quality of thought and practice. Such an advance is unlikely to take place, however, unless power is more equally shared between them and that could be effected by giving Ofsted the statutory duty to explain publicly its response to honest feedback and to the increasing fragmentation of the national system.

One further reflection concerns the methods employed by researchers in this field. If you interview only senior management, you are likely to end up with a theory about the overwhelming importance of leadership. For what head or principal is going to belittle their own role in transforming institutions and/or the whole system? This approach, however, is likely to downgrade the significance of what happens in classrooms. It is the equivalent of stressing the part played by the bridle and reins and ignoring the fact that it is the shire horses that pull the plough.

The final obstacle is likely to be created by the setting up of hundreds of more 'free' schools and new grammar schools that will further fragment the present system and introduce such unhealthy competition as to destabilize existing partnerships. If ministers insist on measures for which the evidence is overwhelmingly negative, then at the very least there must be independent evaluation to prevent the eventual break-up of the national system of education. These are matters way beyond the remit and control of Ofsted, although reporting on them is not.

Part Three

What are the chances
of reform?

Chapter 5

An organization on the cusp of change

If we want things to stay as they are, things will have to change.

(di Lampedusa, 1960: 31)

5.1 Inspection arrangements and procedures

The quotation above comes from Giuseppe di Lampedusa's novel *The Leopard*. Well, the old leopard of Sicily, the Prince of Lampedusa, wanted to preserve the *status quo* but I do not. Before discussing what room for manoeuvre Ofsted has at its disposal, the scale of the proposed changes needs to be estimated by operationalizing the nine components of the new model, detailed in the previous chapter. Instead of Ofsted's four-point grading scale of 'outstanding', 'good', 'requires improvement' and 'inadequate', the proforma in Table 5.1 invites inspectors to choose a point on a continuum from 'needs a little' to 'needs a lot' of support for each of the nine dimensions. The first dimension, TLA, is given as an example in Table 5.1 where its most effective aspects, according to research (Hattie, 2012; Hattie and Yates, 2014; Coe *et al.*, 2014), are highlighted; and a similar procedure could be adopted for each of the nine dimensions, so that a new inspection report would consist of nine sheets, plus a covering commentary in clear English, free of jargon and accessible to all.

A caveat is needed here about turning the findings of research into simple recipes for schools. Tony Edwards makes the point well:

> ... research can only inform practice because it can never replace other knowledge which teachers bring to bear on practical problems; and that even the best research evidence is not available as fixed, universal relationships between methods and outcomes, but as local, context-sensitive patterns which have to be interpreted by practitioners within their particular working environments.

(Edwards, 2000: 301)

The main advantage of this approach is that it does away with a single adjective – 'outstanding' or 'inadequate' – which can never sum up all the complexities of the extraordinary diversity within either colleges of FE or even within more homogeneous primary schools with fewer specializations, for that matter. Complexity is responded to with complexity. The statistical absurdity and injustice of a single global assessment are done away with and league tables would no longer be able to be drawn up.

At an earlier stage I thought to include an Evaluation Summary Form to present a quick overview of the performance of an institution on the nine components, but strong criticism from some of my friends persuaded me that this was a retrograde step that would contradict my claim above that complexity should be respected. The complexities of TLA and the difficulties of leading and managing large, complex institutions should not be reduced to a superficial summary.

The range of this approach could be extended by substituting the main curriculum areas or departments within a college for the nine dimensions and again inviting inspectors to mark a point on the continuum between 'support' and 'strength' to register their evaluation. No calibration is made along any of the continua to prevent impressionistic judgements being turned into the spurious precision of numbers. The end result will be a more multifaceted and comprehensive summary of the strengths and weaknesses of an institution, together with specific details of the support it needs and where it should come from. Asking inspectors to specify both *What Went Well* and what could be done *Even Better If* is an attempt to pursue one of the main aims of Appreciative Inquiry, which rejects all deficit-based approaches and instead gives pride of place 'to everything that gives life to a system when it is most alive and at its exceptional best' (Cooperrider, 2012: 4). The focus of inspection will also switch from a preoccupation with leadership to an equal focus on classroom teaching and management.

Only when the proformas and the commentary have been completed will the inspectors have access to the institution's data and documents on test and exam results. This deals with the frequently voiced accusation that inspection teams arrive in schools to confirm the conclusions they have drawn from reading the data in advance. If you know what you want to find, you are very likely to find it. An experienced headteacher commented: their pre-judgements 'are virtually impossible to change. It almost makes the inspection itself irrelevant.'[1] This change in procedure would restore a balance between the present obsession with quantitative data and the neglect of a wide range of qualitative features of life in schools.

---

1   Personal communication, 2017.

Table 5.1: Evaluation of TLA

DIMENSION TLA[2]	Choose a point on the continuum to indicate the amount of support needed	
Feedback	A little	A lot
Meta-cognition	A little	A lot
Peer tutoring	A little	A lot
What went well	Even better if	
QUESTIONS	Chosen from the bank of questions to suit the age, specialism and stage of education reached by the students. Questions would clearly be different for pupils in the reception class in a primary school and for students of construction in an FE college.	
Specify support needed		

---

2   The three strategies – feedback, metacognition and peer tutoring – were chosen because research has demonstrated that they have the biggest impact. Research should similarly guide the choice of strategies to be evaluated in the other eight dimensions.

These arrangements will replace Ofsted's practice of making graded judgements on four areas: the effectiveness of leadership and management, which, needless to say, comes first; the quality of TLA; personal development, behaviour and welfare; and outcomes, that is data on qualifications and progress. Inspectors then make a final judgement on overall effectiveness, having in the meantime evaluated the provision for the spiritual, moral, social and cultural development of students.[3] If a judgement of 'inadequate' is made on any one of these areas, then the overall judgement is also likely to be 'inadequate'. This new model offers a way out of this minefield or, to change the metaphor, Damocles had only one sword dangling over his head.

The inspection will be more accurate and effective if an inspector is attached to the institution before, during and after inspection, in order to assess benign and undesirable effects; work with it on agreeing and providing the support it needs; and be part of the team, working alongside inspectorial colleagues (with the specialist expertise the institution needs) and classroom teachers, to implement the recommendations. To show that nothing too radical is being suggested here, the following quotation is taken from the FEFC's framework for inspection for 1993, produced after wide consultation within the FE sector, for the assessment of sixth form and FE colleges:

> Colleges will be invited to nominate a senior member of staff to act as the first point of contact with the inspectorate and to participate in the team inspection by joining team meetings, interpreting evidence and clarifying uncertainties.
>
> (FEFC, 1993: 8)

What was good enough for sixth form and FE colleges in the 1990s should now be resurrected to become part of the inspection of all educational institutions: a link inspector and a college nominee. To ensure that inspectors and college staff are acting as equal partners, the principle of

---

3   A primary school failed its inspection in part because it was said to satisfactorily promote its pupils social and moral but not their spiritual and cultural development. '... no evidence [was] presented to illustrate which observations convinced the inspectors of such finely differentiated effects' (Fitz-Gibbon and Stephenson, 1996: 11). The current inspection handbook lists four criteria for assessing spiritual, three for moral, three for social and five for cultural development. One criterion is quoted in full here to show how far Ofsted's reach now extends: 'The moral development of pupils is shown by their ability to recognise the difference between right and wrong and to readily apply this understanding in their own lives, recognise legal boundaries and, in so doing, respect the civil and criminal law of England' (Ofsted, 2016a: 35). How many hours would be needed to assess this criterion fully and fairly? It is one of 15 such criteria in this sub-area.

50/50 contributions to the dialogue between them, used in peer reviews (Matthews and Headon, 2015), should be adopted. Another feature of the alternative model will be to have the inspection evaluated by both the institution that has been inspected and by the inspectors, using the same notions as discussed earlier in this chapter such as: what went well; even better if; next time the questions should include. If these arrangements are followed, then the final report agreed between the institution and Ofsted would be published to ensure open accountability.

What abilities, experiences and knowledge will be required of inspectors to operate this alternative model? First, their deep and critical knowledge of the research and practice of TLA will have led them to espouse explicit theories of learning, which they will be in the habit of using to enhance their thinking and practice. They will also need recent and relevant teaching and management experience including, for some inspectors, vocational experience of the specialist areas they assess, and for others successful experience of teaching and managing in schools in the toughest areas. Inspectors should be restricted to observing and evaluating those subjects, areas or phases where they have experience and proven competence. A general training in the social sciences and, in particular, in the interpretation of statistics, finances and research evidence, and in the skills of evaluation will also be essential. The outcome should be the type of relationship the teaching profession had with HMI before Ofsted was established: open, genuine and productive dialogue with a cadre of respected and trusted colleagues, acting as the cross-pollinators of challenging questions and ideas, and novel practices and insights.

Ofsted will raise the status of the inspectorate in the eyes of the teaching profession, parents and society more generally by a public commitment to provide the following minimal information, mentioned in the second chapter, in every inspection:

- a justification of the size and representativeness of the sample chosen for evaluation
- a measure of the reliability or consistency of the judgements made
- an assessment of the validity or accuracy of the judgements
- an account after six months, say, of the benign and undesirable effects of inspection.

Table 5.2: Information required by Ofsted before inspection

1. A summary of any school self-evaluation or equivalent
2. The current school improvement plan or equivalent, including any strategic planning that sets out the longer-term vision for the school
3. School timetable, current staff list and times for the school day
4. Any information about pre-planned interruptions to normal school routines during the inspection
5. The single central record of the checks and vetting of all staff working with pupils
6. Records and analysis of exclusions, pupils taken off roll, incidents of poor behaviour and any use of internal isolation
7. Records and analysis of bullying, discriminatory and prejudicial behaviour, either directly or indirectly, including racist, sexist, disability and homophobic bullying, use of derogatory language and racist incidents
8. A list of referrals made to the designated person for safeguarding in the school and those that were subsequently referred to the local authority, along with brief details of the resolution
9. A list of all pupils who are open cases with children's services/social care and for whom there is a multi-agency plan
10. Up-to-date attendance analysis for all groups of pupils
11. Records of the evaluation of the quality of teaching, learning and assessment
12. Information about the school's performance management arrangements, including the most recent performance management outcomes and their relationship to salary progression, in an anonymized format
13. Documented evidence of the work of governors and their priorities, including any written scheme of delegation for an academy in a multi-academy trust
14. Any reports of external evaluation of the school, including any review of governance or use of the pupil premium funding

Source: Ofsted, 2016b: 15

Readers may perhaps be reflecting that these new arrangements are as constricting and cumbersome as Ofsted's current processes. Table 5.2 presents the list of the fourteen types of information required by Ofsted before inspection begins. I could have added the list of 20 different groups of learners that the 'inspectors will pay particular attention to' (Ofsted, 2015b: 6); the list of 14 standards that inspectors must uphold in their work; the list of 10 expectations that Ofsted has of providers; the list of six indicators analysed by inspectors in risk assessment; the list of nine different sets of data to be analysed before inspection; the list of 13 tasks to be carried out by the lead inspector when the college is first contacted; and the list of seven activities inspectors have to carry out at the first meeting with senior management. So far only the first 19 pages from a total of 73 of Ofsted's inspection handbook have been scrutinized for lists, but the point has, I trust, been made. Quantity acquires a quality all of its own. Demanding this amount of data from schools is shifting the burden of proof from the inspectors on to educators. Is it any wonder that a headteacher wrote to me to say: 'I do feel very strongly about the phenomenal waste of staff hours trying to second guess the vagaries and demands of Ofsted rather than spending this time providing a better education for the children in the classroom'.[4]

Another possible objection to the proposed changes is that they would overburden the present cohort of inspectors, to which there are three responses. First, we need to re-establish a more democratic structure of national and local inspection, where Ofsted inspectors work hand in glove with local authority (LA) advisers, who will know their local schools far better than any centrally-based inspectors could ever do, and who could monitor them more closely and less expensively. Inspection will also become more participatory by involving all the principal players in the school's community in peer reviews and formal inspections: not just students, teachers, governors and parents but local employers, local councillors and concerned citizens. These, after all, are the people who are left to pick up the pieces when a school or college is judged to be 'failing', so decisions that have serious consequences, for good or ill for a local community, should be taken by members of that community as part of the inspection team. Ofsted inspectors, with a much broader comprehension of standards across the country, will be well placed to counteract any parochial attitudes on the part of LA advisers. Ted Wragg proposed that the latter 'should be available on secondment to HMI for 20 per cent of their time, one day a week on average, the other 80 per cent being for sustained and regular support, monitoring and advice for schools' (Wragg, 1997: 23). In this way the skills of evaluation will be spread throughout the country.

Second, the multiple remits of Ofsted (see p. 5, fn. 7) are unsustainable. Ofsted needs its responsibilities to be reduced or certain functions (for example, evaluating probation services and education and training in prison), to be hived off to separate specialist organizations. The current overload is a recipe for patchy performance, if not outright failure. Ofsted

---

4   Personal communication, 2017.

should also stop using statutory test data to monitor standards over time. That task should be handed over to an independent body that would use the same secret tests repeatedly on 'samples of pupils of the same age at the same time of year. Testing samples rather than full populations makes the process efficient, and, compared with national testing, a much smaller operation. A secret test is needed because once the content of a test becomes known by teachers it is hard for them ... to keep the ideas in the assessment hidden' (Tymms, 2004: 478).

Third, instead of introducing the alternative model all at once, parts of it could be slowly brought in, step by step, over a number of years in a cumulative process of innovation. Early success and a favourable reception from educators will be assured for instance, by Ofsted publicly accepting: the case for reform; the principles underpinning the new model as set out in Chapter 3; and the arrangements and procedures for inspection outlined at the beginning of this chapter, including access to quantitative data being delayed until the qualitative assessments have been completed. A start could be made by evaluating in the first year only the first three dimensions – TLA, professional learning and democracy – and in each of the two succeeding years another three dimensions could be added to the inspection framework until all nine are being assessed simultaneously.

Let me summarize how I envisage the transformation could get under way. The heart of the proposed model consists of the five principles, the nine dimensions and the attendant questions. Ofsted could set the ball rolling by convening a meeting of all the main players (representatives of the teachers' unions and professional bodies, governors, parents and students) to find out how much support the main features of the model command. The move to consult, to enter into dialogue with the profession would in itself help to restore trustful, working relationships between inspectors and educators. Only when a new, agreed set of principles, dimensions and questions has been settled would it be appropriate to operationalize it; and the specialists in Ofsted would be the best people to tackle that job. In this way, by a slow, careful process of evolution that incorporated the best ideas and arguments as it went along, inspection would become a powerful force for good.

The limitations of the proposed model are openly admitted. I am aware that no football manager's plan survives much longer than the first contact with the opposition. The model is not presented as a final blueprint or a detailed plan, but as the first outline of an alternative approach that is offered as a contribution to the debate on a vital public issue of significance to millions of students, hundreds of thousands of educators and ultimately to the future quality of education in England. It now needs to be peer-reviewed so that it can be modified, refined, made complete, and in the process gather support. A number of topics where I have no expertise – for instance, early years, work experience, apprenticeships, governance and safeguarding – have been omitted and will have to be added by others. If this book sparks off a public debate on Ofsted's principles, methods, effects and future, and gets the needed transformation started, then the effort will have been worth it.

5.2 What room for manoeuvre?

No matter how attractive some of the proposals in the new model may appear to senior management in Ofsted (and they may well be viewed as less than compelling), the task of introducing, sustaining and defending radical reform in a large organization is always daunting. For close on 30 years particular assumptions and practices have developed within Ofsted and staff have become committed to, and knowledgeable about, its benchmarks and grade descriptors. Reform of the kind suggested here will involve staff in considerable extra work so it would be understandable if those staff members who wrote the latest version of the inspection framework and handbook were to resent and resist any changes to procedures that they updated as recently as 2016.

One level of difficulty will be winning internal support for change to Ofsted's organizational culture and traditional patterns of working, but it also has to meet the expectations of ministers and senior civil servants, whose reaction to stories of widespread stress caused by inspection is likely to be one of barely suppressed satisfaction. After all, ministers from all the political parties have over the last 30 years approached reform of the public services with the attitude: 'if it's not hurting, it's not working'. As a motivational device to improve the performance of professionals it leaves much to be desired, but as a means of appearing tough in order to gain votes it is still thought to be a winner by the political class.

What animates this book is the belief that educators could become much more than the current model of inspection allows them to be; that inspection should energize rather than stifle the creativity and autonomy of educators. But how is the transformation to be brought about? What resources can we gather together for a journey of hope? (Williams, 1983).

Eric Olin Wright uses three criteria to evaluate what he calls 'real utopias' (Wright, 2007) – desirability, viability and achievability. *Desirability* in this context requires the proposed change to be upheld by values that are widely shared by the inspectorate and the teaching profession; and that criterion has been met by the five principles set out in Chapter 3. *Viability* focuses on the 'likely dynamics and unintended consequences of the proposal if it were to be implemented' (Wright, 2007: 28) and is a response to the standard objection that proposals for reform can look good on paper, but rarely work in practice. The questions attached to each of the nine components are admittedly incisive and exacting, but they would be in the public domain; they would have been discussed and agreed by the main parties; and answering them would constitute the best programme of staff development that I can think of. The new model will have to be tested in an exploratory trial to ensure that its benign effects far outweigh any possible unintended consequences that are by their very nature difficult to predict. Thirdly, *achievability* asks what practical steps are needed to implement the proposals. This is the most difficult of the three criteria because there are so many uncertainties, even in the short term, but a number of strategies suggest themselves.

First and foremost, the status and autonomy of Ofsted need to be enhanced. It should become a 'buffer' institution between government and educational institutions, on the lines of the now defunct University Grants Committee, to save it from acting (or being thought to act) as the implementer of the transient priorities of government. The inspectorate needs not just to be independent of government but to be widely and accurately *seen* as independent of government. If the principle of keeping government interference at arm's length is thought to be healthy for the nation's finances, as demonstrated by the independence accorded the Bank of England and the Office for Budget Responsibility, then the same autonomy should now be extended to Ofsted for the sake of the nation's education. Politicians would have us believe that they have put students at the heart of the education system. They are not: the state is; and it is time that power was more widely shared.

Is it likely, however, that government, any government, will voluntarily give up power by agreeing to this transformation in Ofsted's status? What will prevent politicians from acting will be not so much the fear of any possible negative effects of radical reform – consider the highly risky experiments being carried out in the National Health Service and in British Universities. Rather, the main impediment to progress is likely to be the deep reluctance of ministers and senior officials to relinquish any power.

What could be done to convince them of the pressing need for change? First, the growing realization that the education system is running ever faster down the wrong road (see Coffield, 2007). Commentators, like the former UK government mental-health champion for schools, Natasha Devon, are now reporting that stress levels among teachers and pupils have become unbearable (Devon, 2017). Explanations of the discrepancy between the increasingly poor performance of English students in international tests and Ofsted's claim of impressive improvements by English schools are wearing thin. What may also help to accelerate support for reform is the building of strategic alliances among those concerned with the current direction of travel. The amalgamation of the two teachers' unions, NUT and ATL, will enable the profession to speak with a more powerful voice and government will have to start listening. Capitalizing on the new social media channels will also help to build pressure for change among parents, governors, employers and all those convinced of the necessity of reform.

There are also welcome signs from within Ofsted of a willingness to listen, to act on the concerns of the profession and to reverse some of the serious misjudgements of the past, such as Sir Michael Wilshaw's absurd claim about FE not being fit for purpose. Witness Sean Harford's comment that 'Ofsted is not an inflexible, immutable organisation' (Harford, 2015: 6). Moreover, in her first interview in January 2017, the new Chief Inspector, Amanda Spielman, posed this question: 'how do we [at Ofsted] make sure we get to the heart of the quality of education in the right way, and in a way that is constructive and adds up to a force for improvement in schools?' (Adams and Weale, 2017). Or consider the appointment of Professor Julius Weinberg, a former vice-chancellor of Kingston University, as the new chair of Ofsted, who replaced the previous chair, David Hoare, the city businessman who told a teachers' conference that the Isle of Wight was blighted by a 'mass of crime, drug problems, huge unemployment and underperforming schools … It's a ghetto. There has been inbreeding' (Weale and Adams, 2016). It can only get better, surely.

We should also take heart from the 'multiple gains' made by independent peer reviews, which have been shown to benefit both the schools reviewed and the schools of those carrying out the reviews (Matthews and Headon, 2015). Some of their more innovative approaches have been incorporated into this new model in Table 5.1, presented earlier in this chapter. These successful peer reviews are located neatly as a halfway house between self-evaluation by schools at one end of the continuum and external Ofsted inspections at the other end. Taken together, self-evaluation, peer reviews and a reformed model of inspection provide some of the essential building blocks needed for a self-improving educational system. The growing number of partnerships that have and are being formed demonstrate the creativity and capacity for collaborative action by educators and will lead to further advances in self-improvement. The ideas proposed here will allow a reformed Ofsted to play a leading role in this transformation that is hopefully so far advanced as to be irreversible.

5.3 Final Comments

The current system of inspection has some merits and performs some functions well, but overall its methods are unreliable, invalid and at times unjust. It is viewed by the majority of educators as an incubus rather than as a catalyst for change. That perception and Ofsted's practices must change if it is to become a force for good. The new model offers a more methodologically sound, just, dignified and democratic form of inspection; it is desirable, viable and achievable. It would clearly reduce Ofsted's power, but the compensation would be to greatly increase its influence and effectiveness.

I used to think that educational research was fulfilling the useful function of speaking truth to power. No longer. Those in power already know, for instance, that the inspection system, for all its positive features, is flawed, dysfunctional and damaging, but they persist with it because they relish their role of 'holding feet to the fire', to use one of their favourite phrases. There is no place in education for such ugly, bullying language and behaviour. Instead, this book offers a fresh look at inspection that brings together what we know about how students, educators, inspectors and whole systems learn best. The system proposed is every bit as tough and exacting as the system it seeks to replace but circumvents its undesirable consequences and failings. The new model will enhance the learning capacity of the system, of Ofsted, of educators and, most importantly of all, of students. Britain – post-Brexit – will need nothing less.

Inspection is a public service, paid for by taxpayers. Ofsted does not belong to the government, to the Department for Education, or to the Inspectorate. It belongs to all those citizens and businesses who pay for it and all those whose lives are affected by it. So, we have not only a right but a duty to review its performance, to point out its deficiencies and to require change when a persuasive case for change has been made. This is the essence of an open, democratic society that offers its citizens the freedom not just to think, but to think differently, on behalf of others.

References

Adams, R. (2017) 'Headteachers urge parents to lobby MPs over school funding cuts'. *The Guardian*, 10 February. Online. www.theguardian.com/education/2017/feb/10/headteachers-urge-parents-to-lobby-mps-over-school-funding-cuts (accessed 5 June 2017).

Adams, R. and Weale, S. (2017) 'New Ofsted chief: "I want everyone to see us as a force for improvement"'. *The Guardian*, 9 January. Online. www.theguardian.com/education/2017/jan/09/ofsted-chief-inspector-schools-amanda-spielman (accessed 5 June 2017).

Alexander, R. (2006) *Towards Dialogic Teaching: Rethinking classroom talk*. 4th ed. Thirsk: Dialogos.

— (2008) *Essays on Pedagogy*. London: Routledge.

— (2010) *Children, Their World, Their Education: Final report and recommendations of the Cambridge Primary Review*. London: Routledge.

Altrichter, H. and Kemethofer, D. (2015) 'Does accountability pressure through school inspections promote school improvement?' *School Effectiveness and School Improvement*, 26 (1), 32–56.

Ball, S.J. (1990) *Politics and Policy Making in Education: Explorations in policy sociology*. London: Routledge.

— (2007) *Education plc: Understanding private sector participation in public sector education*. London: Routledge.

— (2008) *The Education Debate*. Bristol: Policy Press.

— (2017) *Foucault as Educator*. Cham: Springer.

Ball, S.J., Maguire, M., and Braun, A. (2012) *How Schools Do Policy: Policy enactments in secondary schools*. London: Routledge.

Barber, M. and Mourshed, M. (2007) *How the World's Best-Performing School Systems Come Out on Top*. New York: McKinsey and Company.

Becker, H.S. (1967) 'Whose side are we on?' *Social Problems*, 14 (3), 239–47.

Belfield, C., Crawford, C., and Sibieta, L. (2017) *Long-Run Comparisons of Spending per Pupil across Different Stages of Education* (Report R126). London: Institute for Fiscal Studies. Online. www.ifs.org.uk/publications/8937 (accessed 5 June 2017).

Benson, T. (2008) 'Head teacher vulnerability in challenging schools'. In de Waal, A. (ed.) *Inspecting the Inspectorate: Ofsted under scrutiny*. London: Civitas, 27–32.

Black, P. and Wiliam, D. (2009) 'Developing the theory of formative assessment'. *Educational Assessment, Evaluation and Accountability*, 21 (1), 5–31.

Bloom, A. (2017) 'Ofsted chief: Trials show "inspectors make consistent judgements"'. *TES*, 7 March. Online. www.tes.com/news/school-news/breaking-news/ofsted-chief-trials-show-inspectors-make-consistent-judgements (accessed 5 June 2017).

Boothroyd, C. and McNicholas, J. (1997) 'The written evidence'. In Duffy, M. (ed.) *A Better System of Inspection?* Hexham: Office for Standards in Inspection, 7–15.

Brookes, M. (2008) 'We need an inspection process – but not this one'. In de Waal, A. (ed.) *Inspecting the Inspectorate: Ofsted under scrutiny*. London: Civitas, 85–95.

Bruner, J. (1996) *The Culture of Education*. Cambridge, MA: Harvard University Press.

Bushe, G.R. and Kassam, A.F. (2005) 'When is appreciative inquiry transformational? A meta-case analysis'. *Journal of Applied Behavioral Science*, 41 (2), 161–81.

Campbell, D.T. (1976) *Assessing the Impact of Planned Social Change* (Occasional Paper Series No. 8). Hanover, NH: Public Affairs Center, Dartmouth College.

Canning, G. (1798) 'New morality'. *Anti-Jacobin*, 36 (9 July), 623–40 (quote on 630). Online. https://archive.org/details/antijacobinorwe00giffgoog

Coe, R. (2013) 'Ofsted: Part of the problem or part of the solution?' Speech given at the Association of Colleges Annual Conference, Birmingham, 19 November.

Coe, R., Aloisi, C., Higgins, S., and Major, L.E. (2014) *What Makes Great Teaching? Review of the underpinning research*. Durham: CEM/Sutton Trust.

Coffield, F. (2007) *Running Ever Faster down the Wrong Road: An alternative future for education and skills*. London: Institute of Education Press.

— (2008) *Just Suppose Teaching and Learning Became the First Priority ...* London: Learning and Skills Network.

— (2009) *All You Ever Wanted To Know about Learning and Teaching but Were Too Cool To Ask*. London: Learning and Skills Network.

— (2012a) 'Ofsted re-inspected'. *Adults Learning*, 24 (2), 20–1.

— (2012b) 'Why the McKinsey reports will not improve school systems'. *Journal of Education Policy*, 27 (1), 131–49.

— (2013) 'Learning styles: time to move on'. Nottingham: National College for School Leadership. Online. www.nationalcollege.org.uk/cm-mc-lpd-op-coffield.pdf

— (2016) 'Teachers as powerful, democratic professionals'. In Higgins, S. and Coffield, F. (eds) *John Dewey's Democracy and Education: A British tribute*. London: UCL Institute of Education Press, 76–98.

— (2017) 'An open letter to the new chief inspector: "Let's make Ofsted a force for good"'. *TES*, 21 January. Online. www.tes.com/news/further-education/breaking-views/open-letter-new-chief-inspector-lets-make-ofsted-a-force-good (accessed 5 June 2017).

Coffield, F., Costa, C., Müller, W., and Webber, J. (2014) *Beyond Bulimic Learning: Improving teaching in further education*. London: Institute of Education Press.

Coffield, F. and Edwards, T. (eds) (1989) *Working within the Act: Education Reform Act 1988–?* Durham: Educational Publishing Services.

Coffield, F., Moseley, D., Hall, E., and Ecclestone, K. (2004) *Should We Be Using Learning Styles? What research has to say to practice*. London: Learning and Skills Research Centre.

Coffield, F. and Williamson, B. (2012) *From Exam Factories to Communities of Discovery: The democratic route*. London: Institute of Education Press.

Collini, S. (2017a) *Speaking of Universities*. London: Verso.

— (2017b) 'Mayday Manifesto 2017'. *The Guardian Review*, 29 April. Online. www.pressreader.com/uk/the-guardian-review/20170429/281483571277791 (accessed 12 June 2017).

Cooperrider, D.L. (2012) 'What is appreciative inquiry?'. Online. www. davidcooperrider.com/ai-process (accessed 5 June 2017).

Cooperrider, D.L. and Srivastva, S. (1987) 'Appreciative inquiry in organizational life'. *Research in Organizational Change and Development*, 1, 129–69.

Crowley, S. (ed.) (2014) *Challenging Professional Learning*. London: Routledge.

Day, C., Sammons, P., Hopkins, D., Harris, A., Leithwood, K., Gu, Q., and Brown, E. (2010) *10 Strong Claims about Successful School Leadership*. Nottingham: National College for Leadership of Schools and Children's Services.

DES (Department of Education and Science) (1988) *The Curriculum from 5 to 16*. London: HMSO.

Devon, N. (2017) 'Stress among teachers will inevitably cascade downwards towards pupils'. *TES*, 13 February. Online. www.tes.com/news/school-news/breaking-views/stress-among-teachers-will-inevitably-cascade-downwards-towards (accessed 5 June 2017).

de Waal, A. (2008) 'Introduction'. In de Waal, A. (ed.) *Inspecting the Inspectorate: Ofsted under scrutiny*. London: Civitas, 1–14.

Dewey, J. (1916) *Democracy and Education: An introduction to the philosophy of education*. New York: Macmillan.

de Wolf, I.F. and Janssens, F.J.G. (2007) 'Effects and side effects of inspections and accountability in education: An overview of empirical studies'. *Oxford Review of Education*, 33 (3), 379–96.

DfE (Department for Education) (2010) *The Importance of Teaching: The Schools White Paper 2010*. London: Department for Education. Online. www.gov.uk/government/uploads/system/uploads/attachment_data/file/175429/CM-7980.pdf (accessed 5 June 2017).

— (2013) *Teachers' Standards*. London: Department for Education. Online. www.gov.uk/government/publications/teachers-standards (accessed 5 June 2017).

— (2017) *Progress 8 and Attainment 8*. London: Department for Education. Online. www.gov.uk/government/publications/progress-8-school-performance-measure (accessed 5 June 2017).

di Lampedusa, G. (1960) *The Leopard*. Trans. Colquhoun, A. London: Collins and Harvill Press.

Drucker, P.F. (1994) *Post-Capitalist Society*. Oxford: Butterworth-Heinemann.

Duffy, M. (ed.) (1997) *A Better System of Inspection?* Hexham: Office for Standards in Inspection.

Earle, J., Moran, C., and Ward-Perkins, Z. (2017) *The Econocracy: The perils of leaving economics to the experts*. Manchester: Manchester University Press.

Earley, P. (1998) 'Conclusion: Towards self-assessment?' In Earley, P. (ed.) *School Improvement after Inspection? School and LEA responses*. London: SAGE Publications, 168–76.

Edwards, T. (1989) 'The National Curriculum: Entitlement or division?' In Coffield, F. and Edwards, T. (eds) *Working within the Act: Education Reform Act 1988–?* Durham: Educational Publishing Services, 2–7.

— (2000) '"All the evidence shows …": Reasonable expectations of educational research'. *Oxford Review of Education*, 26 (3–4), 299–311.

Ehren, M. (2014) 'The International School Inspection Project: Modalities and mechanisms for effective school inspection'. Keynote presentation given at the ISI-TL Symposium, University of Gothenburg, 3 June.

Evans, Bernie (2016) letter, *The Guardian*, 23 December.

FEFC (Further Education Funding Council) (1993) *Assessing Achievement* (Circular 93/28). London: Further Education Funding Council.

Fielding, M. (2001) 'Ofsted, inspection and the betrayal of democracy'. *Journal of Philosophy of Education*, 35 (4), 695–709.

— (2016) 'Why and how schools might live democracy as "an inclusive human order"'. In Higgins, S. and Coffield, F. (eds) *John Dewey's Democracy and Education: A British tribute*. London: UCL Institute of Education Press, 114–30.

Fielding, M., Bragg, S., Craig, J., Cunningham, I., Eraut, M., Gillinson, S., Horne, M., Robinson, C., and Thorp, J. (2005) *Factors Influencing the Transfer of Good Practice* (Research Brief RB615). London: Department for Education and Skills.

Fielding, M., Elliott, J., Burton, C., Robinson, C., and Samuels, J. (2006) *Less is More? The development of a schools-within-schools approach to education on a human scale at Bishops Park College, Clacton, Essex*. Brighton: Centre for Educational Innovation.

Fielding, M. and Moss, P. (2011) *Radical Education and the Common School: A democratic alternative*. London: Routledge.

Fitz-Gibbon, C. (1993a) *Ofsted, Schmofsted*. Newcastle: CEM Centre, School of Education. Online. www.cem.org/attachments/publications/CEMWeb031%20Ofsted%20Schmofsted.pdf

— (1993b) *Performance Indicators for FEFC Inspection*. Newcastle: CEM Centre, School of Education.

— (1996) 'Judgements must be credible and fair'. *Times Educational Supplement*, 29 March, 21.

— (1997) 'Ofsted's Methodology'. In Duffy, M. (ed.) *A Better System of Inspection?* Hexham: Office for Standards in Inspection, 16–20.

— (1998) Memorandum submitted to House of Commons Education Sub-Committee, November. Online. www.publications.parliament.uk/pa/cm199899/cmselect/cmeduemp/62/8111103.htm

Fitz-Gibbon, C.T. and Stephenson, N.J. (1996) 'Inspecting Her Majesty's Inspectors: Should social science and social policy cohere?' Paper presented at the European Conference on Educational Research, University of Seville, 25–8 September.

Gaertner, H., Wurster, S., and Pant, H.A. (2014) 'The effect of school inspections on school improvement'. *School Effectiveness and School Improvement*, 25 (4), 489–508.

Gardner, H. (1993) *The Unschooled Mind: How children think and how schools should teach*. London: Fontana.

Gilbert, C. (2012) *Towards a Self-Improving System: The role of school accountability*. Nottingham: National College for School Leadership.

Gouldner, A.W. (1968) 'The sociologist as partisan: Sociology and the welfare state'. *American Sociologist*, 3 (2), 103–16.

Gray, J. and Wilcox, B. (1995) 'The methodologies of school inspection: Issues and dilemmas'. In Brighouse, T. and Moon, B. (eds) *School Inspection*. London: Pitman, 127–42.

Grosz, S. (2013) *The Examined Life: How we lose and find ourselves*. London: Chatto and Windus.

Harford, S. (2015) Speech given at the Association of School and College Leaders Conference, 20 March. Online. www.gov.uk/government/speeches/speech-to-association-of-school-and-college-leaders-conference-2015 (accessed 5 June 2017).

Hargreaves, D.H. (1995) 'Inspection and school improvement'. *Cambridge Journal of Education*, 25 (1), 117–25.

— (2004) *Learning for Life: The foundations for lifelong learning*. Bristol: Policy Press.

— (2010) *Creating a Self-Improving School System*. Nottingham: National College for Leadership of Schools and Children's Services.

— (2011*) Leading a Self-Improving School System*. Nottingham: National College for School Leadership.

— (2012*) A Self-Improving School System: Towards maturity*. Nottingham: National College for School Leadership.

Harris, A. (2004) 'Distributed leadership and school improvement: Leading or misleading?' *Educational Management Administration and Leadership*, 32 (1), 11–24.

Hartley, D. (2010a) 'Book review: Distributed Leadership According to the Evidence'. *Educational Management Administration and Leadership*, 38 (1), 138–40.

— (2010b) 'Paradigms: How far does research in distributed leadership "stretch"?' *Educational Management Administration and Leadership*, 38 (3), 271–85.

Hattie, J. (2012) *Visible Learning for Teachers: Maximizing impact on learning*. London: Routledge.

Hattie, J. and Yates, G.C.R. (2014) *Visible Learning and the Science of How We Learn*. London: Routledge.

Havel, V. (1978) *The Power of the Powerless*. Trans. Wilson, P. Online. www.vaclavhavel.cz/showtrans.php?cat=eseje&val=2_aj_eseje.html&typ=HTML (accessed 5 June 2017).

Hind, D. (2008) *The Threat to Reason: How the Enlightenment was hijacked and how we can reclaim it*. London: Verso.

Jones, G. (2017) 'Amanda Spielman is wrong – Ofsted should never be seen as a "force for improvement"'. *The Telegraph*, 13 January. Online. www.telegraph.co.uk/education/2017/01/13/amanda-spielman-wrong-ofsted-should-never-seen-force-improvement/ (accessed 5 June 2017).

Jones, K. and Tymms, P. (2014) 'Ofsted's role in promoting school improvement: The mechanisms of the school inspection system in England'. *Oxford Review of Education*, 40 (3), 315–30.

Leithwood, K., Day, C., Sammons, P., Harris, A., and Hopkins, D. (2006) *Seven Strong Claims about Successful School Leadership*. Nottingham: National College for School Leadership.

Lift Off (2016) *Summary Report*. Online. Download from www.asdan.org.uk/courses/programmes/lift-off (accessed 12 June 2017).

Louis, É. (2017) 'Édouard Louis: "For my family, a book was a kind of assault"'. *The Guardian*, 11 February. Online. www.theguardian.com/books/2017/feb/11/edouard-louis-books-assult-elite-working-classes-culture (accessed 5 June 2017).

MacBeath, J. (2008) 'A new relationship with schools?' In de Waal, A. (ed.) *Inspecting the Inspectorate: Ofsted under scrutiny*. London: Civitas, 33–41.

— (2009) 'Distributed Leadership: Paradigms, policy, and paradox'. In Leithwood, K., Mascall, B., and Strauss, T. (eds) *Distributed Leadership According to the Evidence*. London: Routledge, 41–57.

Mansell, W. (2007) *Education by Numbers: The tyranny of testing*. London: Politico's Publishing.

— (2008) 'Ofsted: Overseeing the tyranny of testing'. In de Waal, A. (ed.) *Inspecting the Inspectorate: Ofsted under scrutiny*. London: Civitas, 53–68.

— (2017) 'Where did all the GCSE pupils go – and why has no one noticed?' *The Guardian*, 21 March. Online. www.theguardian.com/education/2017/mar/21/gcse-pupils-secondary-schools-lost-ofsted (accessed 5 June 2017).

Maslow, A.H. (1999) *Toward a Psychology of Being*. 3rd ed. New York: John Wiley and Sons.

Matthews, P. and Headon, M. (2015) *Multiple Gains: An independent evaluation of Challenge Partners' peer reviews of schools*. London: Institute of Education Press.

Matthews, P. and Sammons, P. (2005) 'Survival of the weakest: The differential improvement of schools causing concern in England'. *London Review of Education*, 3 (2), 159–76.

McInerney, L. (2016) 'Farewell, Sir Michael Wilshaw, the Dirty Harry of Ofsted'. *The Guardian*, 20 December. Online. www.theguardian.com/education/2016/dec/20/michael-wilshaw-ofsted-chief-inspector-schools (accessed 9 June 2017).

Moss, G. (2007a) 'Understanding the limits of top-down management: Literacy policy as a telling case'. In Coffield, F., Steer, R., Allen, R., Vignoles, A., Moss, G., and Vincent, C. *Public Sector Reform: Principles for improving the education system* (Bedford Way Papers). London: Institute of Education Press, 19–33.

— (2007b) 'Lessons from the National Literacy Strategy'. Paper presented at the British Educational Research Association Annual Conference, London, 8 September.

Mourshed, M., Chijioke, C., and Barber, M. (2010) *How the World's Most Improved School Systems Keep Getting Better*. New York: McKinsey and Company.

Newby, M. (1998) Memorandum submitted to House of Commons Education Sub-Committee, November. Online. www.publications.parliament.uk/pa/cm199899/cmselect/cmeduemp/62/8111104.htm

Ofsted (Office for Standards in Education) (1995) *The Annual Report of Her Majesty's Chief Inspector of Schools, 1993/94*. London: HMSO.

Ofsted (Office for Standards in Education, Children's Services and Skills) (2012) *The Annual Report of Her Majesty's Chief Inspector of Education, Children's Services and Skills, 2011/12*. London: The Stationery Office.

— (2014) *Raising Standards, Improving Lives: Ofsted's Strategic Plan 2014 to 2016*. Manchester: Ofsted. Online. www.ofsted.gov.uk/resources/140128 (accessed 5 June 2017).

— (2015a) *Investigation: School leaders' views on the impact of inspection*. Manchester: Ofsted. Online. www.gov.uk/government/publications/school-leaders-views-on-the-impact-of-inspection (accessed 5 June 2017).

— (2015b) *The Common Inspection Framework: Education, skills and early years*. Manchester: Ofsted. Online. www.gov.uk/government/publications/common-inspection-framework-education-skills-and-early-years-from-september-2015 (accessed 5 June 2017).

— (2016a) 'Ofsted inspections: Myths'. Online. www.gov.uk/government/ publications/school-inspection-handbook-from-september-2015/ofsted-inspections-mythbusting (accessed 5 June 2017).

— (2016b) *School Inspection Handbook*. Manchester: Ofsted. Online. www.gov. uk/government/uploads/system/uploads/attachment_data/file/553942/School_ inspection_handbook-section_5.pdf (accessed 5 June 2017).

— (2017) *'Do Two Inspectors Inspecting the Same School Make Consistent Decisions?' A study of the reliability of Ofsted's new short inspections.* Manchester: Ofsted. Online. www.gov.uk/government/publications/do-two-inspectors-inspecting-the-same-school-make-consistent-decisions (accessed 5 June 2017).

Ofstin (Office for Standards in Inspection) (1996) *Improving School Inspection: An account of the Ofstin Conference, New College, Oxford, 19–21 June 1996.* Hexham: Office for Standards in Inspection.

O'Leary, M. (2017) 'Introduction: Reclaiming lesson observation as a tool for teacher learning'. In O'Leary, M. (ed.) *Reclaiming Lesson Observation: Supporting excellence in teacher learning.* London: Routledge, 1–9.

Ouston, J. and Davies, J. (1998) 'Ofsted and afterwards? Schools' responses to inspection'. In Earley, P. (ed.) *School Improvement after Inspection? School and LEA responses.* London: SAGE Publications, 13–24.

Perry, P. (2008) 'From HMI to Ofsted'. In de Waal, A. (ed.) *Inspecting the Inspectorate: Ofsted under scrutiny.* London: Civitas, 42–52.

Pinker, S. (2014) *The Sense of Style: The thinking person's guide to writing in the 21st century.* London: Allen Lane.

Power, M. (1997) *The Audit Society: Rituals of verification.* Oxford: Oxford University Press.

Raeside, C. (2017) 'Christine Raeside, Senior HMI, on checking the quality of an inspection'. Ofsted blog, 15 March. Online. https://educationinspection.blog. gov.uk/2017/03/15/christine-raeside-senior-hmi-on-checking-the-quality-of-an-inspection/ (accessed 5 June 2017).

Rose, C., Rose, P., and Galbraith, N. (2016) *Building for Progression: A foot on the ladder.* Bristol: ASDAN.

Sartre, J.-P. (1955) *No Exit, and Three Other Plays: The Flies, Dirty Hands, The Respectful Prostitute.* New York: Vintage Books.

Searle, J. and Tymms, P. (2007) 'The impact of headteachers on the performance and attitudes of pupils'. In O'Shaughnessy, J. (ed.) *The Leadership Effect: Can headteachers make a difference?* London: Policy Exchange, 18–42.

Sennett, R. (2012) *Together: The rituals, pleasures and politics of cooperation.* London: Allen Lane.

Smithers, R. (2005) 'Woodhead overrode inspectors to fail improving school'. *The Guardian*, 4 February. Online. www.theguardian.com/uk/2005/feb/04/politics. freedomofinformation (accessed 5 June 2017).

Spielman, A. (2017) 'A new direction'. Speech given at the Association of Colleges Ofsted Conference, 17 March. Online. www.gov.uk/government/speeches/ amanda-spielman (accessed 5 June 2017).

Stoll, L. and Louis, K.S. (eds) (2007) *Professional Learning Communities: Divergence, depth and dilemmas.* Maidenhead: Open University Press.

Stratton-Berkessel, R. (2015) 'Appreciative inquiry: Overview of method, principles and applications'. Online. http://positivitystrategist.com/appreciative-inquiry-overview/ (accessed 5 June 2017).

Tan, C.Y. (2016) 'Examining school leadership effects on student achievement: The role of contextual challenges and constraints'. *Cambridge Journal of Education*, 1–25.

Timperley, H. (2011) *Realizing the Power of Professional Learning*. Maidenhead: Open University Press.

Tymms, P. (1997) 'High stakes in Ofsted inspections'. *Times Higher Education Supplement*, 19 December. Online. www.timeshighereducation.com/news/high-stakes-in-ofsted-inspections/105063.article (accessed 5 June 2017).

— (2004) 'Are standards rising in English primary schools?' *British Educational Research Journal*, 30 (4), 477–94.

Vaughan, R. (2015) 'Ofsted purges 40% of inspectors'. *TES*, 19 June. Online. www.tes.com/news/school-news/breaking-news/ofsted-purges-40-inspectors (accessed 5 June 2017).

Watkins, C. (2005) *Classrooms as Learning Communities: What's in it for schools?* London: Routledge.

Weale, S. and Adams, R. (2016) 'Ofsted's David Hoare quits under pressure over Isle of Wight slur'. *The Guardian*, 23 August. Online. www.theguardian.com/education/2016/aug/23/ofsted-chair-david-hoare-quits-after-isle-of-wight-ghetto-remarks (accessed 5 June 2017).

Wilde, O. (1966) *Complete Works of Oscar Wilde*. New ed. London: Collins.

Wiliam, D. (2008) 'The Education Reform Act: 20 years on'. Presentation given at Institute of Education conference, London, June. Online. Download from www.dylanwiliam.org/Dylan_Wiliams_website/Presentations.html (accessed 5 June 2017).

— (2011) *Embedded Formative Assessment*. Bloomington, IN: Solution Tree.

Williams, R. (1983) *Towards 2000*. London: Chatto and Windus.

Wilshaw, M. (2012) 'High expectation, no excuses'. Speech given at the London Leadership Strategy "Good to Great" Conference, 9 February. Online. www.gov.uk/government/news/high-expectation-no-excuses (accessed 5 June 2017).

— (2016) 'The power of education'. Speech given at the launch of Ofsted's 2015/16 Annual Report. Online. www.gov.uk/government/speeches/the-power-of-education (accessed 5 June 2017).

Wolf, A. (2007) 'Putting managers in their place'. In O'Shaughnessy, J. (ed.) *The Leadership Effect: Can headteachers make a difference?* London: Policy Exchange, 50–6.

Wragg, T. (1997) 'Inspection and school self-evaluation'. In Duffy, M. (ed.) *A Better System of Inspection?* Hexham: Office for Standards in Inspection, 21–5.

Wright, E.O. (2007) 'Guidelines for envisioning real utopias'. *Soundings*, 36, 26–39.

Wulf, A. (2015) *The Invention of Nature: The adventures of Alexander von Humboldt, the lost hero of science*. London: John Murray.

Index